LaVILLE ELEMENTARY SCHOOL

DORLING KINDERSLEY  EYEWITNESS BOOKS

TRAIN

Jigsaw puzzle featuring Thomas the Tank Engine

Midland Railway coat of arms

Railroad ticket

Model of 1843 Norris locomotive

Signal tower bell tapper

Preserved 1938 steam locomotive *Duchess of Hamilton*

EYEWITNESS BOOKS

TRAIN

Metal whistle

Written by

JOHN COILEY

Columbine steam locomotive, 1845

Railroad police batons

French railroad pass

Dorling Kindersley

Model of U.S. steam locomotive, 1875

Royal train headlight

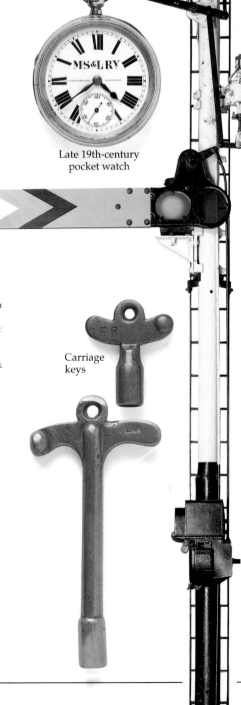

Mechanical semaphore signal

Late 19th-century pocket watch

Carriage keys

Passenger tickets

DK

Dorling Kindersley

LONDON, NEW YORK, AUCKLAND, DELHI, JOHANNESBURG, MUNICH, PARIS and SYDNEY

For a full catalog, visit

DK www.dk.com

Project editor Christine Webb
Art editor Ann Cannings
Managing editor Helen Parker
Managing art editor Julia Harris
Production Louise Barratt
Picture research Cynthia Hole
Special photography Mike Dunning

© 1992 Dorling Kindersley Limited
This edition © 2000 Dorling Kindersley Limited
First American edition, 1992

Published in the United States by
Dorling Kindersley Publishing, Inc.
375 Hudson Street,
New York, NY 10014
6 8 10 9 7 5

Dorling Kindersley books are available at special discounts for bulk purchases for sales promotions or premiums. Special editions, including personalized covers, excerpts of existing guides, and corporate imprints can be created in large quantities for specific needs. For more information, contact Special Markets Dept.

Library of Congress Cataloging-in-Publication Data
Coiley, John.
Train / written by John Coiley;
special photography by Mike Dunning.
p. cm. — (Eyewitness Books)
Includes index.
Summary: Traces the development of railways from the first Babylonian rutways to the electromagnetic, driverless trains of today and describes how trains are built and operated.
l. Railroads—Juvenile literature. [l. Railroads.]
l. Dunning, Mike, ill. II. Title.
TF148.C56 2000 625.1—dc20 92-4711
ISBN 0-7894-5757-1 (pb)
ISBN 0-7894-5756-3 (hc)

Color reproduction by Colourscan, Singapore
Printed in China by Toppan Printing Co. (Shenzhen) Ltd.

Station handbell

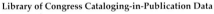

Contents

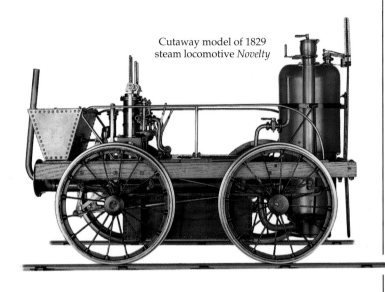

Cutaway model of 1829
steam locomotive *Novelty*

What is a train?

A TRAIN IS ONE OR MORE VEHICLES that ride on wheels and travel along a track. It is pulled by a locomotive or is self-propelled. Trains, and railroads of one form or another, were used long before the first steam locomotive came into existence. The earliest trains relied on human power to push or pull them along the tracks. Horses were even stronger than people and could pull heavier loads. But it was the invention of the steam locomotive that enabled the potential of the railroad to be fully appreciated. Steam trains were far more powerful. With smoother, stronger tracks, they could run faster, hauling both people and freight. Starting with the first steam locomotive in the early 1800s, the railroad advanced rapidly. With the help of modern engineering techniques, diesel and electric locomotives are still improving the quality of the railroad today.

MUSCLE POWER
The earliest railroads were built for private use, such as in mines. When longer public lines had to be constructed, armies of workers were needed, since very little specialized equipment was available. The workers, sometimes known as "navvies," had to dig and shift soil, lay tracks, and build bridges and tunnels using hand tools and sheer muscle power.

DAY TRIPPERS
Steam trains had become a familiar sight by the end of the 19th century. They made it possible for people living in the country near big cities to commute into the city for work, or for pleasure. Similarly, city-dwellers could enjoy a trip to the countryside or the seaside.

A reproduction of an 1830 first-class car from the Liverpool and Manchester line in Britain

LIVERPOOL HUSKISSON MANCHESTER
RAILWAY — COMPANY

Tracks

DIESEL TRAINS
The first successful diesel trains were introduced in the 1930s on passenger services in Europe and the U.S. Ten years later, diesel-electric locomotives were replacing even the largest steam locomotives. The days of steam were almost over. Today diesel power is used worldwide (pp. 40–41).

PASSENGER TRAINS
Huge numbers of passengers travel on the railroads every day. Passenger trains have developed significantly from the early days of the 1820s and 1830s, when many cars were little more than open wagons with seats (pp. 28–29). Passenger cars were gradually equipped with lighting, heating, and restrooms. For longer journeys, sleeping and dining cars were provided.

ELECTRIC TRAINS
Electric trains first ran on a subway in the 1890s (pp. 56–57). They take their power from overhead cables, or from a live (elecrified) rail on the track. Electric trains are faster, quieter, and cleaner, without the pollution produced by diesel or steam locomotives. Most new railroads, whether between or within cities, are likely to be electric (pp. 38–39).

LOCOMOTIVE POWER
Trains carry passengers or freight – and sometimes both. They run on tracks and have wheels with a flange, or lip, that sits inside the rails. The first trains, like this modern reproduction, were hauled by steam locomotives. Nowadays, most trains are hauled by diesel or electric locomotives.

MOVING GOODS
The earliest trains were built to move freight – mainly coal. Today, railroads remain an important method of moving freight, though traffic in most countries has declined dramatically due to competition from road transportation.

A reproduction of Robert Stephenson's Rocket locomotive of 1829

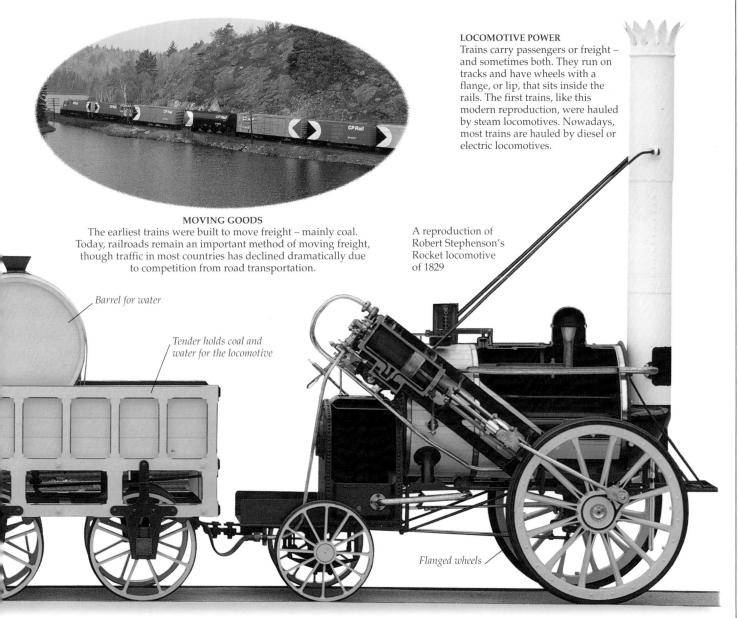

Barrel for water

Tender holds coal and water for the locomotive

Flanged wheels

The first railroads

RAILROADS EXISTED LONG BEFORE steam engines were invented. The railroads that we know today developed from ones first used in European mines in the mid-16th century. To make manual work easier, heavy loads were transported in wagons with four wheels. These wagons ran on parallel wood planks. A peg fixed under the wagon fit into a slot between the planks. This guided the wagon. Later railroads had different guiding systems. Some had rails with flanges, or lips, that kept the wheels from slipping off. Others had smooth rails, and the wheels had a flange to keep them on the rails (pp. 24–25). Until the steam locomotive came along, the main means of hauling the loads was either human power or horsepower.

ANCIENT ROADWAYS
Evidence of tracks built to guide vehicles traveling along them – the basic principle of a railroad – can still be found in Mediterranean countries. Early civilizations, such as the Babylonians and the Sumerians, were aware of the benefits of roadways made out of stone slabs. Because these roadways had uneven surfaces, grooves were cut in the stone to help guide the vehicles. Grooved stone tracks made by the Romans can still be seen in the ruins of Pompeii (above).

EASY RIDER
Some of the earliest railroads in Britain were used to transport coal from coal mines to ships on the nearby rivers. In general, much of this journey was downhill, and a brakesman had to control the wagon's descent. To conserve their energy for pulling the empty wagons back up the hill to the mine, many horses had a ride downhill in a special wagon, such as this one known as a "dandy cart."

This dandy cart was used to transport a horse downhill

STAGECOACH
The stage coach was the fastest means of transportation before the railroads. By using relays of horses, stage coaches and fast mail coaches could travel at an average speed of about 7 mph (11.3 kph).

HUMAN POWER
This engraving, published in 1752, was the first illustration of an English railroad. The railroad was apparently hand-operated. It is also the first recorded use of a flanged wheel on a railroad in Britain.

HEAVY LOADS
This English railroad was built in 1815 and was used for transporting supplies of domestic coal. Its rails were made of cast iron. Horses were used to pull the wagons, which were fitted with flanged wheels.

JAPANESE HORSEPOWER
Horse-powered railroads were widely used throughout the world for pulling vehicles with passengers or freight until the early 1900s, and in some cases long afterward.

DELIVERING COAL
Loaded chaldrons, or coal wagons, descended by gravity to their destination point. This brakesman can be seen controlling the wagon's speed by sitting on the handle of a simple lever brake, while the horse follows behind.

EARLY GERMAN RAILROADS
Although horses had been used to pull loads on wagon roads in Germany since the 18th century, the first steam railroad in Germany did not open until 1835 (pp. 16–17).

A wagon-load of coal became a measure of coal known as a "chaldron"

CHALDRON
"Chaldron" was the name given to the wood wagon used to carry coal from coal mines to the Tyne River in the northeast of England, where the coal was further transported by sea. The chaldron was loaded from above at the mine. When on the wooden wharf (platform) over the river, it discharged coal through a door in the floor, directly into a ship waiting below.

Brake lever

Flanged wheel

Dawn of the steam age

The first practical steam engines were designed by Thomas Newcomen in 1712 and James Watt in 1769. Other engineers tried to use this steam power to drive self-propelled vehicles. The first vehicle of this kind was difficult to control and caused such an uproar in the streets of Paris that the project was abandoned. It was not until the early 19th century that the first successful guided railroad locomotives were designed, though there were still many technical problems to overcome. The engines had to be powerful enough to pull a heavy load, but make as little noise and smoke as possible. They also had to run on smooth rails that would not break under their weight, rails that the wheels could grip without slipping.

LOCAL ATTRACTION
This engraving shows a locomotive built in 1808 by Richard Trevithick. It pulled a four-wheeled car around a circular track and was open to the public. This was the first steam locomotive to run in London. Because of the circular track, the locomotive became known as "Catch me who can."

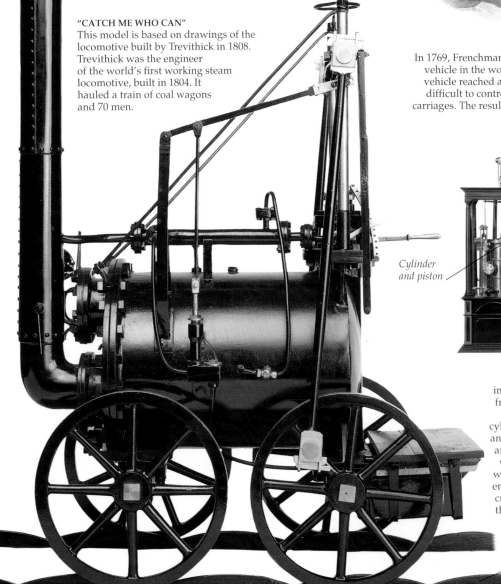

"CATCH ME WHO CAN"
This model is based on drawings of the locomotive built by Trevithick in 1808. Trevithick was the engineer of the world's first working steam locomotive, built in 1804. It hauled a train of coal wagons and 70 men.

THE FIRST ATTEMPT
In 1769, Frenchman Nicholas Cugnot built the first self-propelled vehicle in the world. His three-wheeled steam-powered road vehicle reached a speed of 9 mph (14.5 kph). However, it was difficult to control in a street full of people and horse-drawn carriages. The resulting uproar led Cugnot to abandon the project.

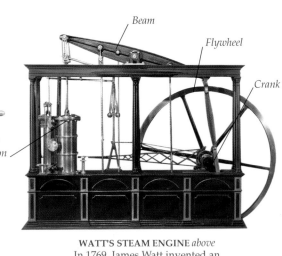

Beam

Flywheel

Crank

Cylinder and piston

WATT'S STEAM ENGINE *above*
In 1769, James Watt invented an improved steam engine to pump water from mines. Steam was used to push a large piston to the top of a sealed cylinder. The steam was then condensed, and air pressure forced the piston down, and the cycle was repeated. The piston was connected to one end of a beam, which rocked back and forth. The other end of the beam turned a flywheel via a crank. This power was used to operate the water pumps. Such an engine was, however, far too heavy and cumbersome for a locomotive.

Flanged rails for guiding smooth wheels

BY LAND AND BY WATER
The first self-propelled land vehicle in the U.S. was this scow (a type of boat), built by the blacksmith and boatbuilder Oliver Evans in 1804. It ran on wheels under its own steam. When it reached water, the wheels were removed and it continued its journey as a propeller-driven boat.

GETTING A GRIP
In their search for the perfect locomotive, early engineers tried to improve the grip of the wheels on the rails. In this 1812 engraving the locomotive's driving wheel fits onto a toothed rack running alongside the smooth rails, giving extra grip.

CHAOS
This 1828 cartoon was an artist's impression of what the streets of London might have looked like with the coming of steam-powered road vehicles.

Puffing Billy is one of the two oldest surviving steam locomotives in the world

PUFFING BILLY
Puffing Billy was built by William Hedley in Wylam, northern England, in 1813. It was used to haul coal wagons from a mine to a nearby river, a distance of about 5 miles (8 km). It proved that, with the right design, there was sufficient grip between a smooth driving wheel and a smooth rail for a locomotive to pull a commercial load. Because of complaints about the noise and smoke that it made, *Puffing Billy* was modified so that the steam passed through a "quieting" chamber before going up the smokestack.

Fuel supply

Coal shovel used on *Puffing Billy*

The engineer stood here

Steam locomotives come of age

Polish stamp showing a locomotive built by Robert Stephenson

It was the vision of Englishman George Stephenson, the "father of railways," that led the way to the age of steam. Stephenson saw that the steam locomotive was the way forward for the railroads. Together with his son Robert, he established his locomotive works in 1823 and began to build steam locomotives for Britain and other countries around the world. By the mid-19th century, the steam locomotive had been adopted worldwide by virtue of its strength, simplicity, and reliability. The basic principles of the steam locomotive's design remained essentially unchanged until diesel-electric and electric locomotives signaled the end of the age of steam (pp. 38–41).

STEAM FOR THE PEOPLE
The Stockton and Darlington Railway opened in England in 1825 and was the world's first public railroad to use steam from the start. At first, the locomotives on this line were reserved for freight trains. It was not until 1833 that they were used for passenger trains.

BEST FRIEND OF CHARLESTON
The *Best Friend of Charleston* was the first successful steam locomotive to be built in the U.S. The *Best Friend* entered service in 1830 and operated the first regular steam service in the U.S.

Engraved ivory pass c. 1830

Railroad directors were provided with free lifetime passes

Gold and enamel pass c. 1850

NOVELTY
In 1829, the Rainhill trials were held to choose a locomotive design for the new Liverpool and Manchester Railway in England. Huge crowds gathered to see the entrants. One of them was *Novelty*. It was a very fast engine but broke down too frequently.

Cutaway model of *Novelty*

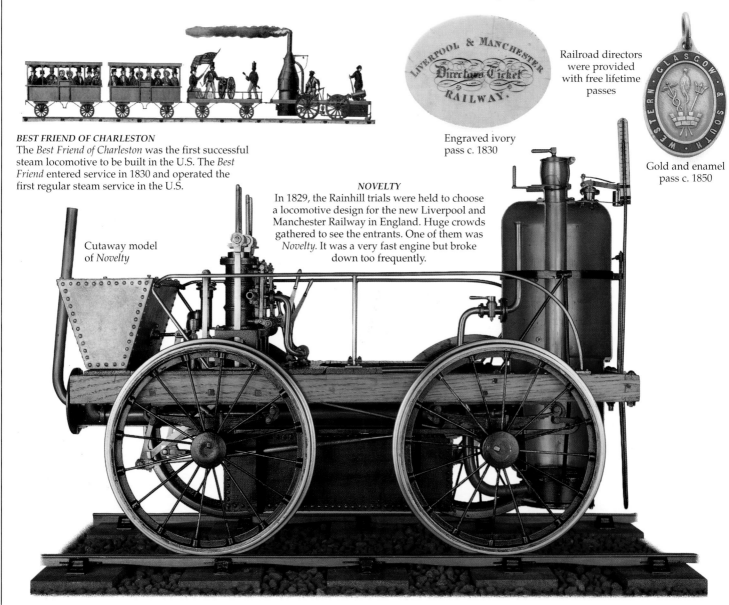

STEAM REACHES EUROPE
After the success of the Liverpool and Manchester Railway, steam railways were soon adopted all over Europe. This print shows a scene on the first railroad between Leipzig and Dresden in Germany in 1837.

AMERICAN CLASSICS
The steam passenger train was established in the U.S. by the mid-19th century. American locomotives could not be mistaken – they had large headlights, wood "cowcatchers" for keeping animals off the line, and bronze warning bells.

Robert Stephenson

FLYING SCOTSMAN
By the 1920s, famous express trains ran throughout the world. One of the most famous was the *Flying Scotsman* express, which traveled 392.7 miles (633 km) between London and Edinburgh, Scotland.

Rocket locomotive, built in 1829

WINNER TAKES ALL
Rocket is one of the most famous locomotives in the world. It entered the 1829 Rainhill trials and won the competition. In doing so it established, once and for all, the superiority of the steam locomotive over the horse as a means of power for railroads. It was Robert Stephenson who was largely responsible for the design of *Rocket*.

How a steam locomotive works

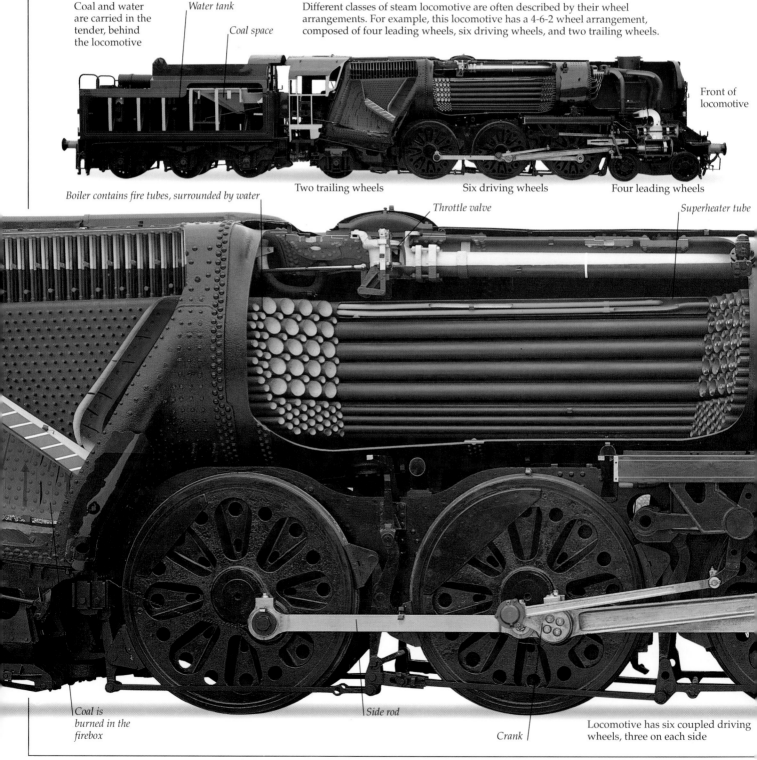

T HE DESIGN OF ALL STEAM LOCOMOTIVES is based on the same principles that governed the building of the very first ones. First, a fire in the firebox heats up water in the boiler, producing steam. This steam is used to move a piston back and forth. The movement of the piston turns the wheels via a connecting rod and crank.

U.S. steam locomotive

Coal and water are carried in the tender, behind the locomotive

Water tank

Coal space

WHEEL ARRANGEMENTS
Different classes of steam locomotive are often described by their wheel arrangements. For example, this locomotive has a 4-6-2 wheel arrangement, composed of four leading wheels, six driving wheels, and two trailing wheels.

Front of locomotive

Boiler contains fire tubes, surrounded by water

Two trailing wheels

Six driving wheels

Four leading wheels

Throttle valve

Superheater tube

Coal is burned in the firebox

Side rod

Crank

Locomotive has six coupled driving wheels, three on each side

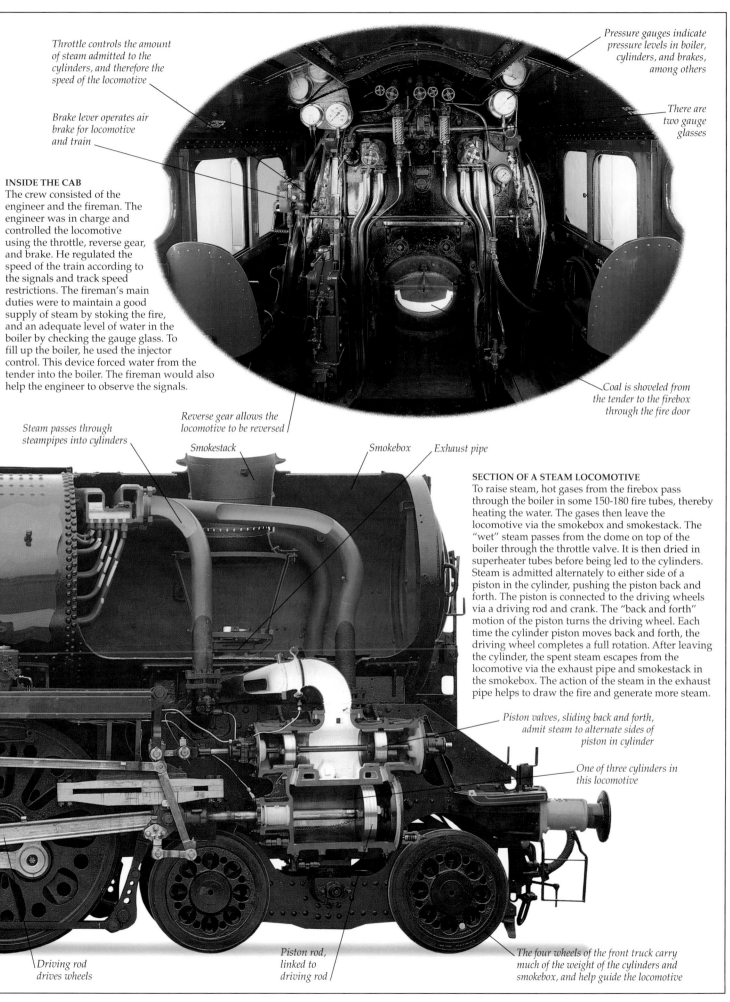

Throttle controls the amount of steam admitted to the cylinders, and therefore the speed of the locomotive

Brake lever operates air brake for locomotive and train

Pressure gauges indicate pressure levels in boiler, cylinders, and brakes, among others

There are two gauge glasses

INSIDE THE CAB

The crew consisted of the engineer and the fireman. The engineer was in charge and controlled the locomotive using the throttle, reverse gear, and brake. He regulated the speed of the train according to the signals and track speed restrictions. The fireman's main duties were to maintain a good supply of steam by stoking the fire, and an adequate level of water in the boiler by checking the gauge glass. To fill up the boiler, he used the injector control. This device forced water from the tender into the boiler. The fireman would also help the engineer to observe the signals.

Coal is shoveled from the tender to the firebox through the fire door

Reverse gear allows the locomotive to be reversed

Steam passes through steampipes into cylinders

Smokestack

Smokebox

Exhaust pipe

SECTION OF A STEAM LOCOMOTIVE

To raise steam, hot gases from the firebox pass through the boiler in some 150-180 fire tubes, thereby heating the water. The gases then leave the locomotive via the smokebox and smokestack. The "wet" steam passes from the dome on top of the boiler through the throttle valve. It is then dried in superheater tubes before being led to the cylinders. Steam is admitted alternately to either side of a piston in the cylinder, pushing the piston back and forth. The piston is connected to the driving wheels via a driving rod and crank. The "back and forth" motion of the piston turns the driving wheel. Each time the cylinder piston moves back and forth, the driving wheel completes a full rotation. After leaving the cylinder, the spent steam escapes from the locomotive via the exhaust pipe and smokestack in the smokebox. The action of the steam in the exhaust pipe helps to draw the fire and generate more steam.

Piston valves, sliding back and forth, admit steam to alternate sides of piston in cylinder

One of three cylinders in this locomotive

Driving rod drives wheels

Piston rod, linked to driving rod

The four wheels of the front truck carry much of the weight of the cylinders and smokebox, and help guide the locomotive

Railroads reach the world

THE OPENING OF THE FIRST "modern" railroad in England, in 1830, aroused interest all over the world. People from many countries came to see it and travel on it. When other countries set up their own railroads, many chose to follow British designs for locomotives, cars, and track. At first, equipment was made in Britain. Each country started to modify the designs to build their own equipment. By the mid-1830s, the U.S. was even exporting steam locomotives to Europe. The railroads had a great impact on all aspects of life from trade to travel. In the U.S., for example, they spanned the vast distances that had been a barrier to opening up the continent (pp. 18–19).

GERMANY'S FIRST
The first steam-operated railroad in Germany was opened in 1835 between Nuremberg and Fürth on a line 5 miles (8 km) long. The English-built locomotive, seen here, was called *Der Adler*.

INDIAN LOCOMOTIVE
The strong British influence in India until 1947 meant that much rail equipment, including locomotives and cars, was supplied from Britain. This model shows a typical design of steam locomotive built in Britain for use on the East Indian Railways. Details such as the sun blinds on the cab windows and the large headlight were specially added.

ASIAN RAILROADS
The first steam-worked railway line in Japan opened in 1872. This 19th-century woodblock contrasts modern transport technology of the time – the steam locomotive – with Japan's traditional forms of transport, such as horse-drawn and human-drawn carriages.

Handrail

Power unit

PARISIAN STEAM
The opening of public railroads aroused much interest. This painting shows the first public steam railroad in France, which opened in 1837. The line ran northwest from Paris to Le Pecq.

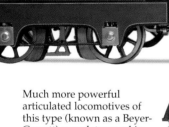

CUSTOM-BUILT
This powerful locomotive was designed and built in Britain in the mid-1930s, for use on the Chinese National Railway. The locomotive is wider and higher than would be possible for use in Britain or Europe. The tender is very large, as it had to carry as much water and coal as possible to work heavy trains over long distances.

MADE IN THE USA
This locomotive model is of a design by William Norris of Philadelphia, built in 1843 and exported to Austria. It was specially designed to work on lines with steep inclines and sharp curves.

FOR EXPORT
This locomotive was built in Britain in 1909 for use in Tasmania. It was the first of a new type of articulated (composed of segments) locomotive, designed for use on lines with sharp curves. Powerful locomotives of this type were made up of two steam power units pivoted at either end of the main frame, which carries the boiler and the cab.

Much more powerful articulated locomotives of this type (known as a Beyer-Garratt) were later used in countries in Africa, as well as in India, Australia, and Britain

The American railroad

FEW NATIONS have had their history and development influenced so greatly by a new mode of transportation as the U.S. In Europe the new railroads were made to serve existing cities, but in the U.S. the railroads themselves created many of the centers of population, in what had been a huge, relatively empty continent. Progress was rapid. By 1869, people could cross the continent by rail. In the early 20th century, most North Americans lived within 25 miles (40 km) of a railroad. Since then, the fortunes of the railroads have declined, largely as a result of competition from road and air transportation. Nowadays, there are signs of a rail revival in areas where the electric railroad has helped to cut down on city road congestion and pollution.

"THE GOLDEN SPIKE"
On May 10, 1869, the U.S. was finally crossed by a railroad from east to west when the last spike, made of gold, was driven at Promontory, Utah, to join the Union Pacific Railroad to the Central Pacific Railroad.

A tall smokestack improved the draft of the fire and made the locomotive more efficient – but there could be no low bridges on the line!

TOM THUMB
In 1830, *Tom Thumb*, a small experimental locomotive, made its first run on the 13-mile (21-km) completed section of the Baltimore and Ohio Railroad. *Tom Thumb* also entered into a celebrated race, seen here, with a horse-drawn train. The horse won.

IT'S A FIRST
The *Stourbridge Lion*, the first steam locomotive with flanged wheels to run on rails in the U.S., was built in England in 1829. It was very similar to *Agenoria* (above), which was built for use in England.

Wheel has flange, or lip

Engineer's cab

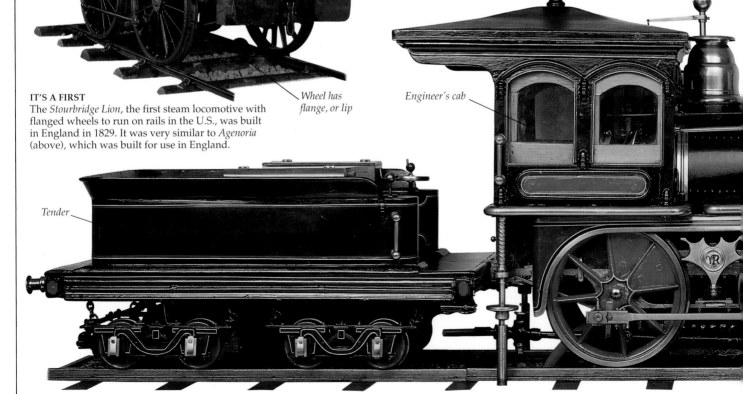

Tender

DE WITT CLINTON
The first steam train in New York State was hauled by the locomotive *De Witt Clinton* on August 9, 1831. The cars were little more than stagecoaches. Passengers rode on top of the vehicles, as well as inside.

BUILDING THE FUTURE
The opening up of the continent by the spread of the railroad was recognized as a great achievement with tremendous potential. Railroads were to play an important part in the growth, and wealth, of many towns across the U.S.

TROUBLESOME TIMES
During the construction of lines westward, trains were sometimes attacked by Native American Indians. These were not unprovoked attacks – the Indians were trying to defend their way of life, which was under threat. The developers who appeared with the spread of the railroads were taking their land and hunting grounds from them.

Pivoted, or moving, axle

Cowcatcher keeps animals from derailing the locomotive

JOHN BULL
This was an early four-wheeled locomotive, designed by Robert Stephenson. It was shipped in sections from England in 1831. The *John Bull* soon displayed a tendency to derail, and so became the first locomotive to be fitted with a two-wheeled pivoted axle in front of the driving wheels, together with a "cowcatcher."

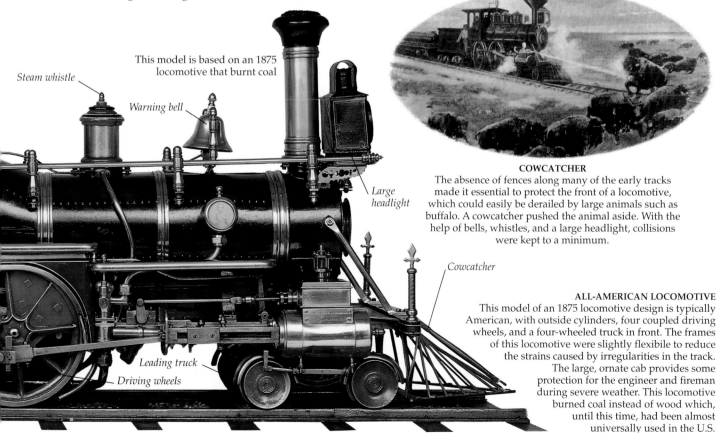

This model is based on an 1875 locomotive that burnt coal

Steam whistle

Warning bell

Large headlight

Cowcatcher

Leading truck

Driving wheels

COWCATCHER
The absence of fences along many of the early tracks made it essential to protect the front of a locomotive, which could easily be derailed by large animals such as buffalo. A cowcatcher pushed the animal aside. With the help of bells, whistles, and a large headlight, collisions were kept to a minimum.

ALL-AMERICAN LOCOMOTIVE
This model of an 1875 locomotive design is typically American, with outside cylinders, four coupled driving wheels, and a four-wheeled truck in front. The frames of this locomotive were slightly flexibile to reduce the strains caused by irregularities in the track. The large, ornate cab provides some protection for the engineer and fireman during severe weather. This locomotive burned coal instead of wood which, until this time, had been almost universally used in the U.S.

Building the railroads

Workman's pick

F$_{AR\ MORE\ WORK}$ goes into building a railroad than might be expected. Since trains cannot climb steep hills, it may not be possible to build in a direct line between two places. Trains often have to follow longer, less hilly routes. To keep the railroad route as level as possible, embankments and cuts have to be made, and bridges and tunnels built. The engineer in charge selects the route by deciding what the steepest gradient, or slope, can be. The type of trains that will use the railroad and the balance between speed and load have to be taken into account. Very steep gradients can be avoided by spreading the route with "S" curves or spirals. To avoid making the route too long, tunnels and bridges may be built. These are expensive, but provide a much shorter and more level route.

SIMPLE TOOLS
The most basic tools, such as this pick, were used to build early railroads. Other equipment included shovels, shoulder hods (for carrying bricks), wheelbarrows, simple hoists, and wood scaffolding. Gunpowder was used to blast the way through solid rock. The large number of "navvies," or workmen, lived in makeshift temporary accommodations near the site.

BLOOD, SWEAT, AND TEARS
Early cuts through rock, such as this 1831 example, were excavated with only primitive hand tools. A large workforce was needed, and the work took many years to complete. Much of the rock recovered was used to make stone ties on other railroads.

THE CONSTRUCTION CREW
In the 19th century, U.S. railroads were usually built by crews living on site, in cars pulled by steam locomotives. The train would move the crews along the line as it was completed; it would also provide steam heating and hot water. Supplies and new rails were brought to the end of the line by other trains. Earth and rocks excavated from cuts were often used to build embankments. The wood trestle shown in the picture would have been built using local supplies.

Construction crew, 1885

BUILDING BRIDGES
When a bridge is built over a river, a temporary island of rocks must first be made in the middle, or posts driven into the riverbed. Construction of the bridge can then begin. The parts of the bridge are floated down the river into position. This early wooden arch bridge was built on wood piers. The arch is shaped so that it counterbalances the point where the bridge will bend most under a heavy load. This design of bridge has been used extensively by the railroads.

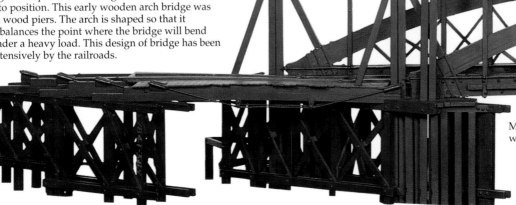

Model of 1848 wooden arch bridge

BRIDGES FOR TRAINS

There are many kinds of railroad bridges each with a specific use, depending on the local geography. Cantilever bridges are used when a large span – for example, over water – is needed. Beam bridges arose from the simple concept of a tree trunk across a stream. These bridges usually have several supporting solid masonry piers. Trestles, made from timber or steel, are similar to beam bridges. Arch bridges have a curved support on which the section carrying the track rests. Some bridges, such as the Royal Albert Bridge near Plymouth, England (left), are based not on one, but on a mixture of bridge designs.

Royal Albert Bridge, near Plymouth, designed by Brunel in 1859

CHANNEL TUNNEL

Building a tunnel under the sea is a major feat of modern engineering. The Channel Tunnel provides a rail link between Britain and France (pp. 62–63). The tunnel is 31 miles (49.8 km) long and is 24 miles (38.6 km) under the sea. Construction work is highly automated. Tunnel-boring machines the diameter of the tunnel worked toward one another from both sides of the channel. After the tunnels joined, the machines were buried, since it was too difficult to remove them. The tunnel opened to passenger trains in 1994.

BRUNEL
Isambard Kingdom Brunel (1806–1859) was an outstanding mechanical and civil engineer. He was responsible for designing many of the great railroads, bridges, and tunnels in Britain.

WHO PAYS?

Many railroads have been financed by government-issued stocks and bonds. Governments support the railroads, as they are of both commercial and military importance. This gold bond certificate was issued in 1872 by the U.S. government to finance railroad construction. In many countries the railroads have been taken over by the state, or maintained with a large government subsidy.

COMING AND GOING
Passenger stations (pp. 48–49) are designed to help the arrival and departure of passengers and to provide services while they are using the station.

Bridges on major rivers had to be high enough so that ships could pass underneath

Overcoming obstacles

AS RAILROAD SYSTEMS GREW, more and more attention had to be given to the obstacles that limited or prevented their further development. At first these obstacles were mainly physical barriers along the proposed route – such as deep valleys, hills and mountains, and wide rivers or lakes. Gradually, as engineering skills and techniques improved, these obstacles were overcome. Tunnels (pp. 20–21) and bridges were built in remote and difficult locations through mountains and over deep valleys and gorges. Railroads were developed that could climb up steep mountains. Today, there are many powerful, high-speed trains on specially built lines that are almost independent of the terrain they travel over. Obstacles to railroad operations and development are now mostly economic and financial.

SYDNEY HARBOR BRIDGE
The Sydney Harbor Bridge is probably best known for its characteristic shape on the Sydney, Australia, skyline. But it is also famous for having the longest steel-arch span in the world – 1,650 ft (503 m). When it opened in 1932, it carried two railroad lines and two tram lines. Now it also carries eight road lanes, a footpath, and a cycle track.

STAYING POWER
Powerful locomotives were required for hauling trains in rugged country with steep grades and tight curves. Normal locomotives of this type were usually long and heavy, which made it very difficult for them to go around the curves. One way around the problem was to adapt the wheels under the locomotive. Swiveling trucks were attached underneath the frame carrying the boiler. This enabled the locomotive to negotiate the tight curves.

Model of Kitson-Meyer tank locomotive built in 1903 for use in Chile

SAIL BY TRAIN
Train ferries have been in use since the middle of the 19th century. Passengers traveling on train ferries do not have to leave the train until they reach their destination.

RIGI RAILWAY
In 1873, a steam-operated railroad was opened to the top of Mt. Rigi near Lucerne, Switzerland, using a rack-and-pinion system to climb steep grades. It was the first such railroad in Europe. A toothed rack was laid between the rails, and a powered cog on the locomotive helped pull the train up the mountain. Working in reverse, it helped to control the train's descent.

TOURIST ATTRACTION
Mountain climbing and sightseeing by steam railroad became a great tourist attraction in the 19th century. The Snowdon Mountain Railway opened in Wales in 1896; it used a rack-and-pinion system to climb the steep mountainsides.

CROSSING WATER
One of the greatest railroad bridges ever constructed, the bridge over the Firth of Forth in Scotland, was opened in 1890. It is the oldest railroad cantilever bridge (pp. 20-21) in the world and is still in use today.

Although this locomotive had one boiler, it had two power units (each with a smokestack), on swiveling trucks. These made it powerful enough for steep uphill stretches.

MOUNT WASHINGTON COG RAILWAY
The world's first mountain rack railroad opened in 1869 in New Hampshire. This line originally used a wrought-iron rack, something like a ladder, which helped the locomotive climb grades that were as much as 10 times steeper than those found on normal railroads.

Swiveling trucks for going around tight curves

Making tracks

RAILS AND TRACKS have been of fundamental importance in the history of trains. Long before the steam locomotive came along, rails were used to guide loaded wagons. However, early rails, made of cast iron, were easily broken. It was not until stronger rails were available that the full potential of the steam locomotive could be exploited. After cast-iron rails came wrought-iron rails, and since the 1870s, steel rails, which are durable and longlasting. Tracks are constantly being improved to meet the requirements of heavier, faster trains. For a smoother ride, most main lines now have continuously welded rails, instead of the jointed short lengths that gave rise to the once-familiar "clickety-clack" of a train journey. The distance between the rails is known as the gauge, and it varies around the world. Some railroads, especially those with difficult terrain to cross, have narrow-gauge lines, which are cheaper and faster to build and maintain.

LAYING TRACKS
Building early railroads was hard work and required large gangs of men working together to lift and position the rails. Little equipment was available, but often there was plentiful cheap labor. Today such work is almost entirely automated.

TRACK MARKS
The track layout at the approach to a busy station can be extremely complex. To enable trains to switch lines, special switches (where trains change tracks) were provided, together with complicated "diamond" crossovers. Nowadays, such track layouts have been simplified, where possible.

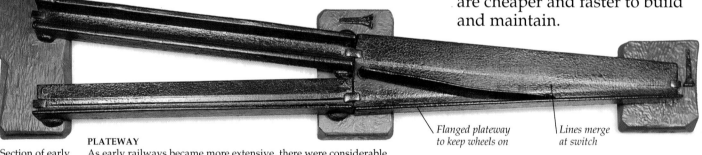

Flanged plateway to keep wheels on

Lines merge at switch

Section of early plateway, 1799

PLATEWAY
As early railways became more extensive, there were considerable benefits in being able to move a wagon from one line to another. This was done by merging two lines at points, or switches. Plateways (above), with their raised flanges, were not easily merged. Plate rail was replaced in the 1820s by smooth-edge rails.

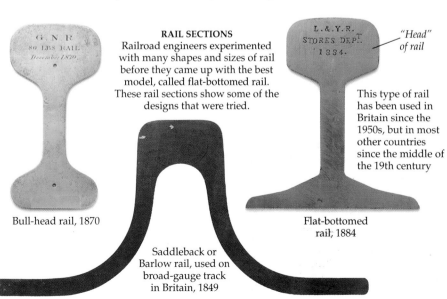

G.N.R
80 LBS RAIL
December 1870.

RAIL SECTIONS
Railroad engineers experimented with many shapes and sizes of rail before they came up with the best model, called flat-bottomed rail. These rail sections show some of the designs that were tried.

L.&.Y.R.
STORES DEPT.
1884.

"Head" of rail

This type of rail has been used in Britain since the 1950s, but in most other countries since the middle of the 19th century

Bull-head rail, 1870

Saddleback or Barlow rail, used on broad-gauge track in Britain, 1849

Flat-bottomed rail, 1884

Outside flange to guide plain wheels (without a flange)

PLATE RAIL
Early rails, such as this plate rail of around 1808, were made in short sections of cast iron and were supported by stone ties.

Flanged wheel fits over plain-edge rail

FISH-BELLY RAILS
These cast-iron rails were designed for extra strength. A deeper section, midway along the rail, was designed to resist the weight of the load.

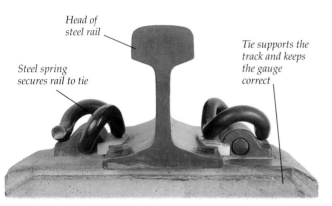

Wood "key" secures rail to chair

Tapered screw fastens chair to tie

Cast-iron chair

Wooden tie

BULLHEAD RAIL
This section of steel bullhead rail was secured in a cast-iron chair by a wood "key." The chair is secured to a wooden tie by large screws.

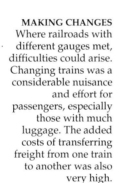

DANGEROUS TIMES
Early filmmakers were fascinated by the dramatic potential of railroads. Here the heroine is being tied to a track consisting of flat-bottomed rails.

Head of steel rail

Tie supports the track and keeps the gauge correct

Steel spring secures rail to tie

FLAT-BOTTOMED RAIL
Modern flat-bottomed rails are made of steel. The rails are secured on a rubber pad, which is fastened to a concrete tie by means of a steel spring assembly. In many places flat-bottomed rails are still fastened directly to a wood tie by a spike.

MAKING CHANGES
Where railroads with different gauges met, difficulties could arise. Changing trains was a considerable nuisance and effort for passengers, especially those with much luggage. The added costs of transferring freight from one train to another was also very high.

F.D. BANISTER Esq, C.E.

GAUGE MEASURE
Special steel measures were used to check the gauge, or distance between rails. The distance was measured from the inside edge of one rail to the inside edge of the other. The standard gauge in North America, and in many other countries including most of Europe, is 4 ft 8.5 in (1435 mm). The broad-gauge measure is wider than the standard gauge, and the narrow-gauge measure is less. However, the actual measurements for each of these gauges varies from country to country.

Freight trains

GO BY RAIL
Bulky loads (such as new road vehicles) have been carried on trains since the 1820s, as shown in this East German stamp.

T‍HE EARLIEST TRAINS were freight trains that carried loads of coal or mineral ores. These trains consisted of only two or three simple wagons and were hauled by a horse. However, with the development of the steam locomotive (pp. 10–11), much longer trains could be operated, and at higher speeds, making rail freight more efficient and economical. As the railway network developed, trains were used to move raw materials to factories and then to distribute the finished products. In the early days, all freight trains were very slow because their primitive brake systems could not stop the train fast enough in case of an emergency. Technical developments since then now mean that freight trains can run at speeds of up to 60 mph (100 kph) or more.

PASSENGERS AND FREIGHT
In the 1830s the first public railroads operated steam-hauled trains for both passengers and freight. A wide variety of freight was carried, including live animals.

LMS
295987   20T

BRAKE VAN
Early freight trains were made up of wagons that did not have brakes. The only means of controlling the train was to apply the brake on the locomotive, and the guard's hand brake on the "brake" van, or caboose. Such brakes were so feeble that in order to control their speed even short trains had to travel no faster than 30 mph (50 kph).

SHEDDING THE LOAD
Most of today's trains are loaded and unloaded automatically, with each train carrying one particular kind of freight. Before this, most freight trains ran with mixed loads. Each wagon contained a different kind of freight. The contents of such "wagon-load" trains were transferred to and from road vehicles at freight depots.

DIESEL POWER
In 1939 in the U.S., the diesel-electric locomotive proved that it could outclass steam. By the mid-1950s most freight trains were hauled by diesel engines.

UNIT

MI

Load not to exceed   Tons   Tare

Specially shaped metal hook

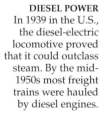

SAFETY FIRST
For many years wagons were joined by three chain links. It was the shunter's job to couple and uncouple the wagons. When doing the job by hand, they risked being injured between the wagons, but they could do it quickly and safely by using a shunter's pole.

Coal wagon from the Stanton coal mine in the north of England

STANTON

9988

TARE 7~4~3

LOAD 12 TONS

Side door for unloading

Hand brake

COAL WAGON
Much of the freight traffic in Britain was made up of coal trains. For many years the coal was carried in simple wagons that were owned by individual coal mines and had a capacity of 10 tons. The wagons were usually automatically loaded from above, but they often had to be unloaded by workers with shovels.

BULK LOADS
Most freight trains now haul bulk loads such as coal, oil, or building materials in specially built wagons. All the wagons are fitted with air brakes operated by the engineer. This means that they can safely run at high speed.

TAILLIGHT
Trains carry a red taillight to indicate that they are complete. This modern electric battery version gives a flashing signal.

ASS **LINED**

D **DAIRIES**

TANK

M*S 44057 SHUNT WITH CARE

MILK TANKER
The coming of the railroads helped to improve the public's diet and health by speedy delivery of milk and produce from rural areas to the cities. By the 1930s milk was being transported in special glass-lined tankers.

First, second, and third class

THE FIRST PUBLIC passenger trains were a far cry from today's comfortable, spacious trains. They offered three different classes of accommodation; those who traveled in the greatest comfort paid the highest fare. First-class accommodation was an enclosed compartment that looked very similar to a stagecoach. It had glass windows and padded seats. Second-class accommodation was an open wagon with seats; the people in the third class had no seats and had to stand or sit on the floor. As passenger trains were improved over the years, the carriages, or cars, were heated and corridors added, giving access to restrooms and to dining cars, as well as making ticket collecting an easier task.

PRIVATE ROOMS
First-class passengers traveled in spacious, comfortable carriages, and they were even able to hold private conversations. Traveling by rail in the second half of the 19th century was regarded as an enjoyable adventure in itself.

American first-class ticket

Australian second-class ticket

British third-class ticket

PAYING THE WAY
Tickets show that passengers have paid for their journey. These tickets look very much like the first card tickets that were made in 1837.

TICKET PUNCH
To indicate that a ticket has been used and inspected, it is "punched," marked, or stamped in some way.

Restroom door

Reading lamp

Comfortable seats

FIRST-CLASS COMPARTMENT
The first-class compartment from the train below has a similar layout to the second- and third-class compartments. But first-class travelers had more legroom and more comfortable and spacious seats. Passengers in this compartment had the smoothest journey, as they were farthest from the bumps and jolts of the wheels.

Third-class compartment

Restroom

EARLY DAYS
The earliest images of steam passenger trains from the 1830s show the enclosed first-class carriages carrying luggage – and guards – on the roof. The second- and third-class vehicles were not enclosed.

Restroom

A FRESH START
The development of railroads and steamships during the 19th century opened the doors to large-scale immigration. This was particularly true in North America once railroads linked the East Coast to the Middle West, and eventually the West Coast. Once they had crossed the Atlantic, immigrants from all over Europe traveled westward on special but very crowded trains.

SECOND-CLASS COMPARTMENT
Compared with first class, this compartment was simpler and had less legroom. Partly because there was very little difference between the second and either the first or third class, the second class almost completely disappeared from trains in Britain soon after this carriage was built.

Posters advertising railway destinations

HARD TIMES
In the early days, third-class travel was a far cry from first-class. Three or four times as many passengers of all ages were crowded into the same space.

CARRIAGE KEYS
When carriages are not in use, they are usually locked for security. The lock is simple and operated by a square-shaped key.

THREE-IN-ONE
This 1904 British carriage (below) is unusual in having first-, second-, and third-class accommodation in the same vehicle, with no connecting corridor. Each compartment had its own restroom. Because there was no corridor connecting this carriage to any other, it could be detached easily from the train.

THIRD-CLASS COMPARTMENT
This compartment had the simplest fixtures and fittings and the least room. However, it was relatively luxurious compared to the hard seats and cramped conditions of the earliest third-class compartments. Located over the wheels, its occupants had the bumpiest and noisiest ride.

First-class compartment

Second-class compartment

Traveling in style

Gold pass allowing directors and senior railway staff free first-class travel

Pullman pass

French pass

Pass for Atchison, Topeka & Santa Fe Railway

BY THE 1850S, the railroads of Europe and the U.S. were offering their passengers such luxurious facilities as heating, lighting, toilets, and catering, especially on long-distance trains. For the railroad companies, the more luxury they offered, the more business they got. In the U.S., businessman George Pullman introduced the first luxury sleeping cars in 1865 and went on to offer first-class dining facilities. Soon afterward, railroad companies with long-distance services started to build hotels alongside their main stations. From then on, the rapid spread of sleeping and dining cars, as well as railroad hotels, made traveling by rail a stylish affair for wealthier passengers.

TOP-NOTCH TRAVELERS
People, such as railroad directors, who held free card passes were able to travel first-class overseas as well as at home.

CHINA AND ROSES
Trains with first-class dining cars served meals on fine china, some of which has since become collectors' items. This breakfast setting was made in the 1930s and has a delicate gilt border with pink roses.

EXCLUSIVE EATING
To those who could afford it, the first-class restaurant car was just as enjoyable as an exclusive restaurant – with the added bonus of a constantly changing view.

TRAVEL A LA MODE
In the 1920s and 1930s the fashionable way to travel was by train. Modern railroads, especially in Europe, still use striking images of elegant travelers from this period to advertise their trains.

ANYONE FOR COCKTAILS?
Even cocktails could be ordered in first-class restaurant cars in Britain in the 1930s. Every railway company had their own monogram, which decorated glasses, silverware, and china.

WHODUNIT? *left*
Famous luxury trains with romantic names have been the setting for many novels and films, including Agatha Christie's *Murder on the Orient Express*.

SYMBOL OF LUXURY *right*
The British Pullman Company coat of arms was carried on the exterior of all Pullman cars. In Britain, Pullman cars operated in one form or another from 1874 until the 1980s.

1960

PULLMAN COMFORT
By the 1870s, American Pullman cars provided all that was needed for a long-distance journey. Travelers could even join in the Sunday hymns. Folded beds can be seen in the background.

Detailed marquetry (inlay) on wood-paneled walls

Bell for calling attendant

PULLMAN STYLE
The interior of the 1914 Pullman car *Topaz* (left) reveals the ultimate in passenger comfort. British-built Pullman cars were renowned for their magnificent detailed woodwork (above). All the seats were armchairs, and each one had a glass-topped table and a brass table lamp in front of it, with a bell beside it for calling the attendant. Meals and refreshments were served at each seat. At each end of this car were private compartments holding four seats, known as coupés.

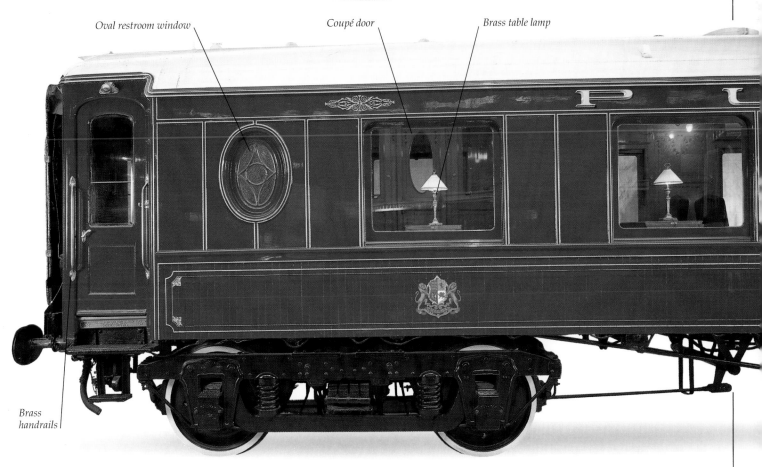

Oval restroom window

Coupé door

Brass table lamp

Brass handrails

In the signal tower

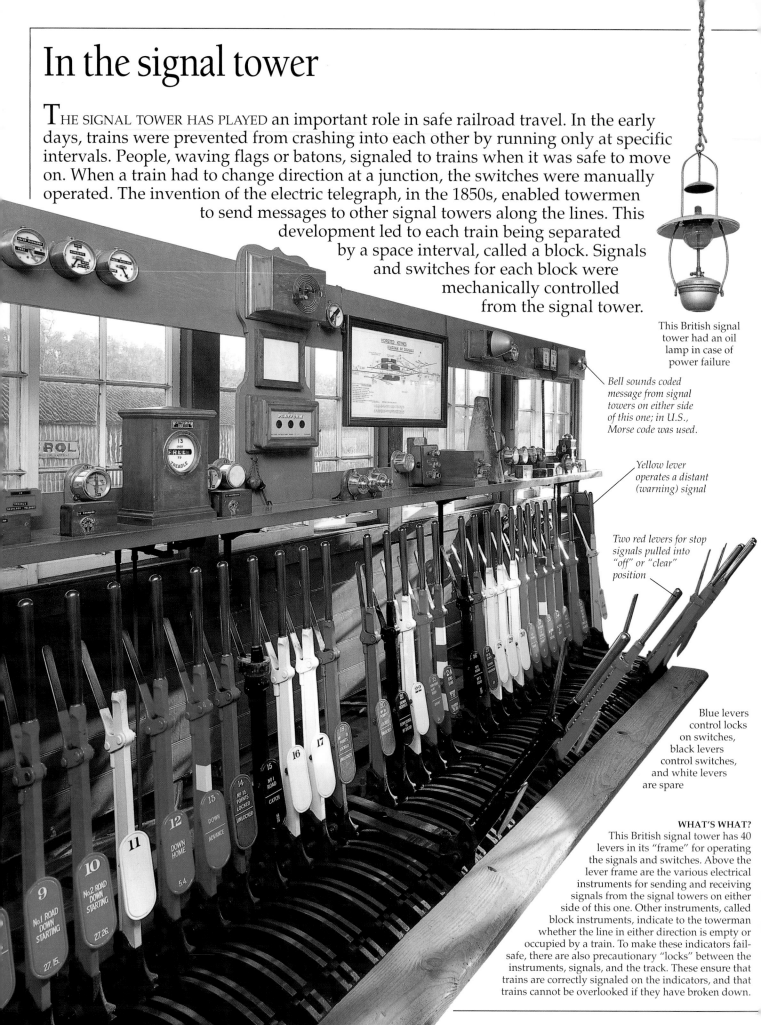

THE SIGNAL TOWER HAS PLAYED an important role in safe railroad travel. In the early days, trains were prevented from crashing into each other by running only at specific intervals. People, waving flags or batons, signaled to trains when it was safe to move on. When a train had to change direction at a junction, the switches were manually operated. The invention of the electric telegraph, in the 1850s, enabled towermen to send messages to other signal towers along the lines. This development led to each train being separated by a space interval, called a block. Signals and switches for each block were mechanically controlled from the signal tower.

This British signal tower had an oil lamp in case of power failure

Bell sounds coded message from signal towers on either side of this one; in U.S., Morse code was used.

Yellow lever operates a distant (warning) signal

Two red levers for stop signals pulled into "off" or "clear" position

Blue levers control locks on switches, black levers control switches, and white levers are spare

WHAT'S WHAT?
This British signal tower has 40 levers in its "frame" for operating the signals and switches. Above the lever frame are the various electrical instruments for sending and receiving signals from the signal towers on either side of this one. Other instruments, called block instruments, indicate to the towerman whether the line in either direction is empty or occupied by a train. To make these indicators fail-safe, there are also precautionary "locks" between the instruments, signals, and the track. These ensure that trains are correctly signaled on the indicators, and that trains cannot be overlooked if they have broken down.

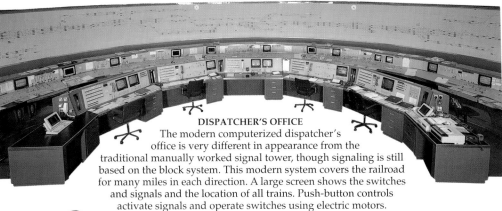

DISPATCHER'S OFFICE
The modern computerized dispatcher's office is very different in appearance from the traditional manually worked signal tower, though signaling is still based on the block system. This modern system covers the railroad for many miles in each direction. A large screen shows the switches and signals and the location of all trains. Push-button controls activate signals and operate switches using electric motors.

THREE-POSITION BLOCK INSTRUMENT
This instrument indicated to the signalman the state of the line between his box and the one before.

ON THE PLATFORM
At many smaller stations in France, the levers for signals and switches were located on the platform. This allowed the station agent to signal trains as well as carry out other duties.

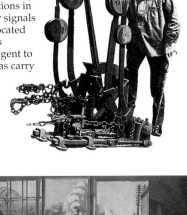

British single-line electric key token instrument

BELL TAPPER
If a British towerman wanted to ask if the next section of line in advance was clear, he used this instrument to send bell codes to the boxes on either side of him.

ALL CLEAR
To operate the switches and signals for each train passing through his block, the towerman had to pull the long levers that were linked to the switches by rods, and to the signals by cables.

Staffs for a journey in the opposite direction were locked into the key token until the line was clear

THE SIGNAL TOWER
Manually operated signal towers in the early 1900s were often raised to accommodate the movement of the lower part of the levers. Today, one dispatcher's office can do the job of dozens of traditional signal towers.

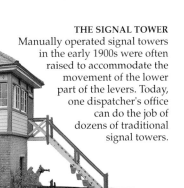

THREE-POSITION PEGGING BLOCK INSTRUMENT
This instrument sent information to the three-position block instrument in the signal tower to the rear. It also displayed the state of the line.

EXTRA PROTECTION
As an added safety measure, British trains on single lines (one track with trains going in both directions) depended on key token instruments. A clear signal could be given only when the engineer had been handed a metal staff.

Following the signs

ENGINEERS ARE FACED with an array of signals along the line. Without signals, they risk colliding with other trains, as often happened in the early days of the railroads. The first engineers obeyed hand signals given by railway policemen. Later, mechanical signals imitated these hand signals. As average train speeds rose and brakes improved, more sophisticated equipment was needed to improve the flow and safety of rail travel. By the 1920s, electric color light signals were being used during both day and night. These lights were much more powerful than the old oil lamps and were much easier to see at a distance, especially at night on fast main lines. All high-speed main lines are now equipped with color light signals, which keep the engineer informed about the state of the line ahead. These signals, and the switches along the track, are all automatically indicated in the signal box.

Red square-ended arm is horizontal, meaning "stop"

STOP THE TRAIN!
At small rural stations, such as this one in Australia, the train stopped only if requested to do so. Passengers wanting to stop the train were told to "wave the tin flag."

Signalman's badge

IDENTIFICATION
On some railroads, workers have always worn badges as part of their uniform, to indicate who they are.

STOP!
This mechanical semaphore signal has two arms. The upper arm indicates whether or not the train should stop, and the lower arm serves as a distant (warning) signal. It tells the engineer whether or not he must stop at the next signal. Here both signals are horizontal and indicate "stop."

SIGNALING LAMP
In the past the conductor would signal to the engineer at the station, using a flag during the day and an oil lamp at night. The glass in this oil lamp could be rotated to give a green (go), red (stop), or white (general use) signal.

Three-aspect conductor's lamp

BATONS AND ARMBANDS
In the early 1840s, railroad policemen acted as signalmen. They would use different colored flags to signal a train to stop, or to proceed with caution, or to show that the line was all clear. They also wore armbands for clear identification and carried ornately decorated batons in case they encountered trouble.

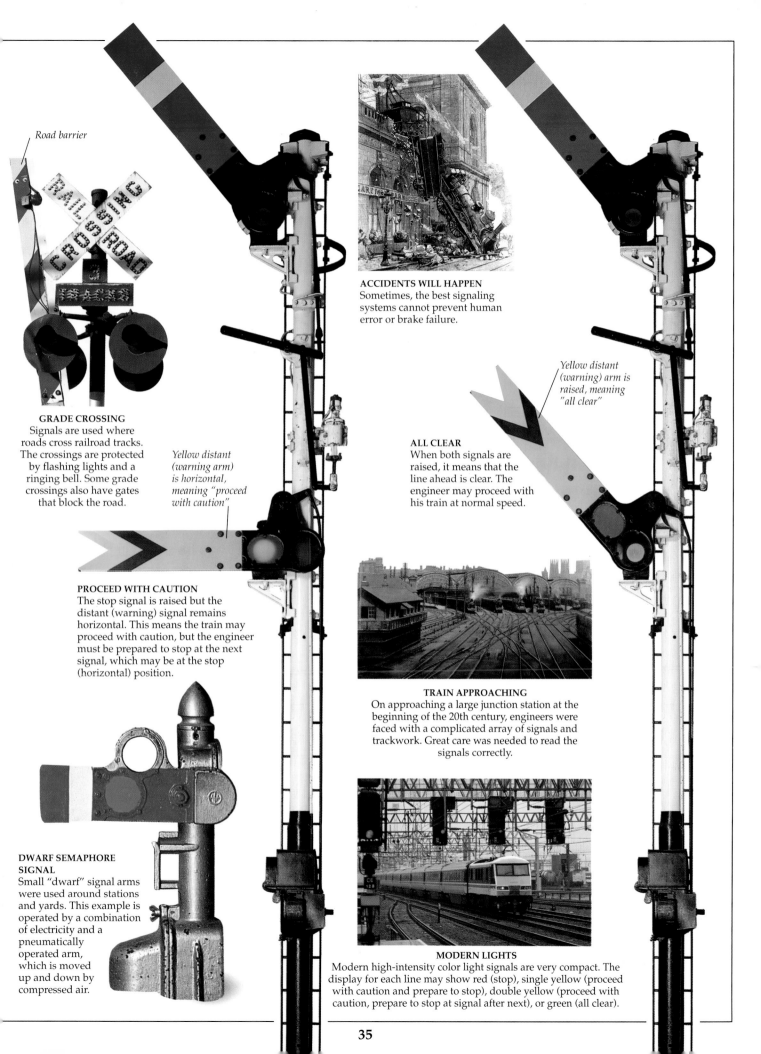

Road barrier

GRADE CROSSING
Signals are used where roads cross railroad tracks. The crossings are protected by flashing lights and a ringing bell. Some grade crossings also have gates that block the road.

Yellow distant (warning arm) is horizontal, meaning "proceed with caution"

PROCEED WITH CAUTION
The stop signal is raised but the distant (warning) signal remains horizontal. This means the train may proceed with caution, but the engineer must be prepared to stop at the next signal, which may be at the stop (horizontal) position.

DWARF SEMAPHORE SIGNAL
Small "dwarf" signal arms were used around stations and yards. This example is operated by a combination of electricity and a pneumatically operated arm, which is moved up and down by compressed air.

ACCIDENTS WILL HAPPEN
Sometimes, the best signaling systems cannot prevent human error or brake failure.

Yellow distant (warning) arm is raised, meaning "all clear"

ALL CLEAR
When both signals are raised, it means that the line ahead is clear. The engineer may proceed with his train at normal speed.

TRAIN APPROACHING
On approaching a large junction station at the beginning of the 20th century, engineers were faced with a complicated array of signals and trackwork. Great care was needed to read the signals correctly.

MODERN LIGHTS
Modern high-intensity color light signals are very compact. The display for each line may show red (stop), single yellow (proceed with caution and prepare to stop), double yellow (proceed with caution, prepare to stop at signal after next), or green (all clear).

Post haste

PICKING UP
This British cigarette card shows local mail, packaged in a leather bag, being picked up at speed by a long-distance Traveling Post Office train.

SOME TRAINS HAD MAIL CARS that were designed to handle all the jobs carried out in a post office while the train sped along. The mail was picked up from specially designed trackside apparatus. Mail clerks then sorted and put it into dispatch sacks for different destinations along the train's route. These sacks were automatically dropped off into trackside nets. The equipment for collecting and dropping off mail was located at one end of the car. The rest of the car was filled with sorting tables, pigeonhole racks, and sacks for sorted mail.

AMERICAN MAIL
This classic American locomotive from the 1870s is hauling a mail train. Mailbags are being thrown out for collection; workers prepare to collect a similar bag hanging from a post as the train passes by.

Mailbox for late letters. Letters delivered here required extra postage

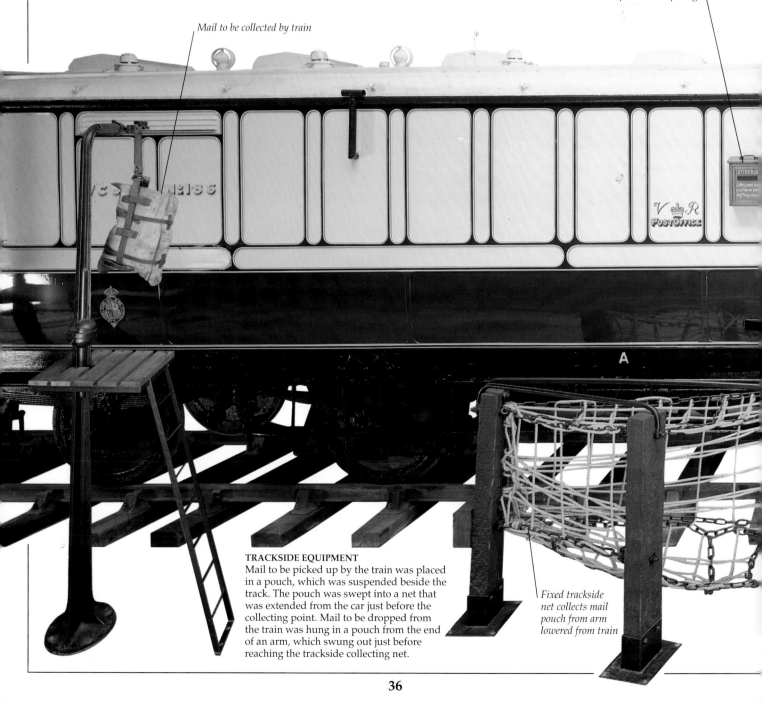

Mail to be collected by train

TRACKSIDE EQUIPMENT
Mail to be picked up by the train was placed in a pouch, which was suspended beside the track. The pouch was swept into a net that was extended from the car just before the collecting point. Mail to be dropped from the train was hung in a pouch from the end of an arm, which swung out just before reaching the trackside collecting net.

Fixed trackside net collects mail pouch from arm lowered from train

ROAD TO RAIL
Sending mail by rail requires cooperation between the railroads and local postal services. Here, the mail car delivers mail to a branch-line station. The local train then takes the mail to a main-line station, where it is put aboard a long-distance passenger train or Traveling Post Office train.

WHAT GOES WHERE?
Incoming mail was emptied from the sacks onto the sorting table (at far left), and individual letters were hand-sorted into pigeonholes. When there were sufficient letters for one destination, they were tied in a bundle and put in a dispatch sack (far right). The sack was dropped off en route, or at the end of the journey.

SWIFTLY BY POST
The "Irish Mail" between London and Holyhead was the oldest named train in the world. It ran from 1848 until 1985, carrying mail from London en route to Dublin. The train also carried passengers, and sleeping accommodations were provided.

Pigeonholes for sorting letters

Net picks up mail bag from lineside

The apparatus for exchanging mail bags from a moving train was last used in the U.S. in the late 1960s and in Britain in 1971

British Traveling Post Office car, 1885

Leather bag with sorted mail to be dropped off

POST OFFICE ON WHEELS
In 1838, with the arrival of a regular railroad passenger service in Britain, it was decided that the Royal Mail should be carried by rail, rather than by fast mail coaches. The railway postal service developed rapidly. In the U.S., the first Railway Post Office came into operation in 1864. The railroads are still used today by mail services around the world, in conjunction with road and air transport.

POST BY RAIL
The strong association between trains and mail is illustrated by this Liberian postal stamp of 1974. The stamp features a modern high-speed experimental tilting train.

Electric trains

THE POTENTIAL OF ELECTRIC POWER was understood in the early days of steam, but people had not yet figured out how to harness this power to drive trains. Engineers developed the first electric trains toward the end of the 19th century, and experimented with varying voltages of electric current. Some locomotives collected power from overhead cables; others took power from a third "live" rail next to the track. Electric locomotives have many advantages over steam and diesel power. They are faster, quieter, and easier to run and maintain. Although building an electric railroad or electrifying an existing one is expensive, electric lines are both economical and efficient. Once built, the extra costs are justified on busy lines such as subways, rapid transit systems, and commuter services.

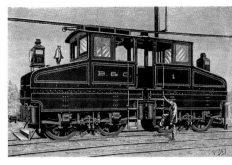

AMERICAN FIRST
The first electric locomotives to be used in the U.S. on a main line were introduced on the Baltimore and Ohio Railroad in 1895 on a section of line (3.75 miles) 6 km long. This short route passed through many tunnels, which had quickly filled with fumes when steam locomotives worked the line.

The pantograph is the "arm" on top of many electric locomotives and trains. It collects the electric current from the overhead power line.

EARLY DAYS OF ELECTRICITY
The first practical electric railroad was designed and operated in 1879 by German engineer Werner von Siemens, at an exhibition in Berlin. His locomotive could pull 30 passengers at a speed of 4 mph (6.5 kph).

LE MISTRAL
This classic French train, which ran until the early 1980s, was pulled by a powerful electric locomotive. It was famed for its comfortable, smooth, high-speed service between Paris and Nice. The stainless-steel cars included a full restaurant car, buffet, and lounge cars.

NORTH

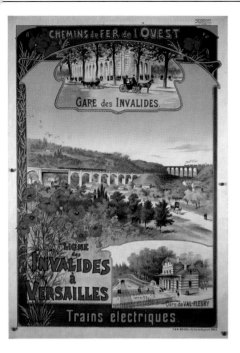

SWIFT AND SAFE
The French railroads used eye-catching posters to advertise their new electric services in the early 1900s. This poster, in the art nouveau style, promoted the fast, clean electric trains running on a local service from Paris to Versailles.

VERY, VERY FAST
The fastest passenger train in the world is the TGV *(Train à Grande Vitesse)*, a French high-speed electric train (pp. 46-47). It runs mostly on specially built tracks that carry no other kinds of train. It runs at an average speed of 132 mph (213 kph) between Paris and Lyons. Each TGV unit is made up of eight cars with an electric locomotive at either end. Its modern design and powerful motors allow the TGV to maintain a high speed, even on steep gradients. This, in turn, allowed special tracks to be built over rather than through the landscape, reducing construction and maintenance costs.

INNOVATIONS
Because of the rapid progress in electrical engineering, even the latest designs for electric locomotives always run the risk of being superseded by better, more advanced designs. This 1991 electric locomotive pulls express trains on the electrified main line between London and Edinburgh, Scotland. However, the cars are designed with future developments in mind. They have sloping sides so that if tilting trains are introduced (pp. 62-63), a major redesign will not be necessary to keep trains clear of each other.

This electric locomotive was built in 1904 by the North Eastern Railway, England

EARLY ELECTRIC LOCOMOTIVE
This electric locomotive was built to replace steam locomotives on a freight line. The line had a badly ventilated tunnel, which quickly filled with choking fumes when worked by steam locomotives. The locomotive was designed to collect the electric current either by overhead pantograph or from a third "live" rail.

Diesel power

THE INVENTION OF THE diesel-powered locomotive, along with the electric locomotive, signaled that the age of steam was drawing to a close. The diesel engine was first demonstrated in 1893 by the German engineer Dr. Rudolph Diesel, who went on to build the first reliable one in the world in 1897. In most diesel locomotives, the engine powers a generator that produces an electric current. This drives electric motors that turn the wheels. Diesel-powered trains are used worldwide, particularly on less busy lines where electrification is not economical.

Rudolph
Diesel

THE DIESEL ENGINE
Unlike a steam engine, a diesel engine does not usually drive the locomotive's wheels directly. Instead, it generates electricity, which then is used to turn the wheels. In the diesel engine, heavy diesel oil is injected into a cylinder of hot, compressed air. The fuel ignites, and the energy released pushes a piston, which drives the generator. The generator makes electricity, which drives a motor that turns the wheels.

Fan cools generator

Generator produces an electric current, which is used to drive the wheels

Diesel engine, which drives generator

Prototype British Rail *Deltic* diesel-electric locomotive, 1956

DELTIC

TRANS-EUROP-EXPRESS
Until the early 1980s, major European cities were linked by an international luxury express service, the TEE, which was particularly useful for businesspeople wanting a fast, reliable, and comfortable intercity service. The diesel-electric trains on these lines catered only to first-class passengers.

"Mash can" for hot drinks

SNACK TIME
Engineers have always had a quick snack and hot drink along the way. The lunch box and "mash can" that British engineers use are similar to those from the days of steam.

Plastic top protects from grease and dirt

DIESEL RECORD
One of the first successful high-speed diesel trains was the *Zephyr* of the Burlington Route, introduced over the 1,000 mile (1,609 km) route from Chicago to Denver in the mid-1930s. In 1936, it set a start-to-stop average speed of 134 kph (83.3 mph), which is still a world record for a sustained rail speed on a run over 1,000 m (1,609 km).

ENGINEER'S CAP
Even though diesel cabs are much cleaner than steam cabs, traditional steam-engine engineers' caps like this one are still worn.

TIME SAVER
High-speed diesel-electric trains, such as this British Rail High-Speed Train, are designed to save time and labor. Instead of the traditional formation of cars hauled by one locomotive, this train has two diesel-electric power cars, one on each end. At the end of the journey, the locomotive does not have to be replaced.

East German stamp featuring a diesel locomotive for switching and for local freight services

PROTOTYPE *DELTIC* LOCOMOTIVE
When this *Deltic* diesel-electric locomotive was built in 1956, it was the most powerful diesel-electric single-unit locomotive in the world. The *Deltic*s successfully replaced the powerful streamlined steam locomotives of the *Mallard* type (pp. 46-47) on Britain's East Coast main line between London and Edinburgh in 1961. In the 20 years that they worked this line, they each ran more than three million miles. Many diesel-electric locomotives have proved to be far more powerful than the steam locomotives that preceded them.

Long distance by train

WHOLE CONTINENTS WERE OPENED UP by the building of long-distance railroads. Early journeys on these railroads were often slow and uncomfortable. But they were an improvement over what, if anything, had been available before. The facilities on long-distance trains slowly improved, particularly in the U.S., with heating, sleeping cars, and eventually restaurant cars being introduced. Today, most businesspeople fly on longer journeys to save time. Long-distance trains, however, remain increasingly popular with tourists. For those who are not in a hurry, traveling by train is an excellent way to see much of a country.

Early sleeping cars had curtains, allowing complete privacy

TRANS-SIBERIAN EXPRESS
The daily passenger train between Moscow and Vladivostok – the *Russia* – makes the longest regular train journey in the world, 5,778 miles (9,297 km), taking seven days in all.

STRAIGHT AND NARROW
The first through-running service from Sydney on the east coast of Australia to Perth on the west coast, was introduced in 1970. The luxury *Indian Pacific* covers the 2,461-mile (3,968-km) route, including the world's longest length of straight track – 297 miles (478 km) – in three days.

BLUE TRAIN
A luxury train has run between Cape Town and Pretoria in South Africa since 1903. In 1939, the *Blue Train* was introduced on this 956 mile (1,540 km) stretch and is now regarded as the most luxurious train in the world.

Containers for tea and coffee

Kettle

Saucepan

Kerosene burner

SNACK TIME
As train speeds increased, the number of station stops for refreshments were cut back or abandoned altogether. Passengers took to bringing their own food in picnic baskets, such as this one containing tea-making equipment. Self-catering on trains remained popular even after the introduction of restaurant cars.

Strap prevented occupant of upper berth from falling out during stormy night passages

Rack for luggage and bedding when bed is folded up

Cupboard containing bottle of drinking water and glass

When covered, washbasin makes a small table

Toilets and washbasins were provided on sleeping cars

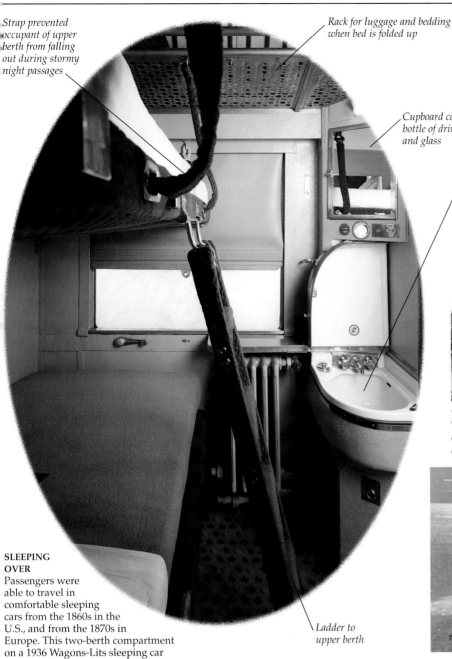

Ladder to upper berth

SLEEPING OVER

Passengers were able to travel in comfortable sleeping cars from the 1860s in the U.S., and from the 1870s in Europe. This two-berth compartment on a 1936 Wagons-Lits sleeping car traveled overnight between London, Paris, and Brussels. When the beds were not in use, the lower berth was converted into seats. Trains on this route crossed the English Channel aboard a train ferry.

WAGONS-LITS CAR

The Wagons-Lits Company was founded in 1876 and operated high-quality sleeping cars and dining cars across Europe, including on the *Orient Express*.

TRAIN FERRY

The Dover-Dunkerque train ferry, linking England with France and the Continent, came into service in 1936. It carried the cars of the trains between London, Paris, and Brussels.

Issued by
The Atchison, Topeka and Santa Fe
Railway Company (Coast Lines)

THE *Super* **CHIEF**

Santa Fe

NON-TRANSFERABLE
PASSENGER'S IDENTIFICATION CHECK

This check should be detached on first presentation of the ticket and returned to passenger who will please retain it as it identifies his transportation.

From LOS ANGELES
To CHICAGO
Train No. 8   JUL 15 1938
(Date)

11442

Form
E. F. 10
Assistant Passenger Traffic Manager
LOS ANGELES, Cal.

Eating lunch in the dining car

Super Chief ticket of 1938

SUPER CHIEF

The *Super Chief* traveled between Chicago and Los Angeles. It established, with the help of gourmet food and a Hollywood clientele, a reputation as the best long-distance train in the U.S.

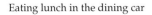

Royal coat of arms on *Gladstone*

Royal trains

Some of the most splendid passenger cars ever built were constructed for the British royal family. Since the first royal railway journey in 1839, members of the royal family have traveled by train when making their longer civic and family journeys around Britain. Trains have offered greater comfort, space, and privacy than road transportation. When built, the royal carriages represented the latest in design, furnishing, and technology. Royal trains are still used today.

GLADSTONE'S LAMP
Oil headlamps on locomotives pulling royal trains were often decorated like this example from *Gladstone*.

ROYAL REGALIA
Locomotives that were used to haul royal trains, like *Gladstone* (above and below), were specially cleaned and prepared. They usually carried elaborate decorations such as cast-metal coats of arms and flags. It is even said that in the 19th century the coal was painted white!

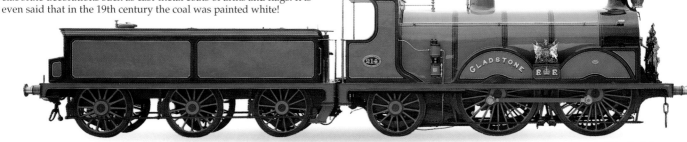

By day the queen sat in the coupé compartment, which had end windows

Attendants' compartment

ROYAL STATIONS
Queen Victoria was an inveterate train traveler and made many civic visits by railway. Some stations were built especially for royal use, such as this one at Gosport, which the queen used when traveling to her residence on the Isle of Wight. The station was richly decorated for her arrival, and she was always greeted with pomp and ceremony.

QUEEN ADELAIDE'S CARRIAGE
The first royal carriage was made for the Dowager Queen Adelaide in 1842. The design was based on three stagecoach compartments and was the state of the art in the field of passenger car construction at the time. The interior was beautifully furnished and upholstered by craftsmen. It is thought that the queen traveled during the day in the end (coupé) compartment, with close attendants in the middle compartment.

QUEEN VICTORIA'S LAVATORY
Much attention was paid to the smallest of rooms. This toilet and washing compartment was beautifully furnished in maple and silk.

QUEEN VICTORIA'S DAY CARRIAGE *above*
No expense was spared when fitting out the royal carriages. The decoration of the day carriage was the personal choice of the queen when it was built in 1869. The wood is bird's-eye maple, the upholstery is blue watered silk, and the ceilings are covered in white quilted silk. The carriage was originally lit with oil lamps, but in 1895 newly developed electric lighting and bells for calling attendants were added. It is said that the queen preferred oil lamps and specially requested that they be kept as well.

KING EDWARD VII'S SMOKING COMPARTMENT
Edward liked to relax in this wood-paneled compartment in his 1902 carriage. It contained the latest electric fans, heaters, and even cigar-lighters.

Sleeping compartment

STRETCHING OUT
At night the queen would transfer from the coupé to the compartment at the other end, where the cushions could be rearranged into a bed. The boxlike extension (the "boot") at the end of the carriage provided extra room for feet and legs.

"Boot" extension

Footrail and step above allowed access from ground level

Wood chassis (framework) with four wheels

QUEEN ALEXANDRA'S BEDROOM
On the wall above the queen's bed were a number of buttons. She could use these to summon any of her servants to her royal bedside during the night.

QUEEN MARY'S DAY COMPARTMENT
The day compartment was one of several compartments in the queen's carriage. She also had a dressing room, bathroom, and bedroom.

Record breakers

Trains have often been involved with spectacle, publicity, and competition – especially in setting speed records. For Britain and the U.S., breaking the speed barrier of 100 miles per hour was a special goal. This goal was reputedly met in 1893, when an American locomotive was claimed to have reached a speed of 112.5 mph (181 kph), and in 1904, when a British locomotive was timed at 102 mph (164 kph). However, serious doubts were subsequently cast on both these claims. From the early days of steam right up to the present day, speed records have been, and still are being, set and broken as countries compete for the absolute record for a standard train.

FAST MOVERS
The first steam engines designed to run at 100 mph (161 kph) on every trip were those of the 1935 *Hiawatha* service, covering 412 miles (663 km) between Chicago and Minneapolis/St. Paul. This service held the world record for the fastest run between two stations on a scheduled service with steam power – it averaged 80 mph (130 kph) over a 78.9 mile (127 km) stretch.

Steam train of the *Hiawatha* service

LNER

ON 3RD JULY 1938 THIS LOCOMOTIVE ATTAINED A WORLD SPEED RECORD FOR STEAM TRACTION OF 126 MILES PER HOUR

THE BEST EVER
The brass plaque attached to the side of *Mallard*'s boiler commemorates the world speed record for a steam locomotive set on July 3, 1938.

Mallard is a streamlined Pacific-type steam locomotive built by the London North Eastern Railway at Doncaster in 1938

R 4468

LIKE A BULLET

When opened in 1964, the Japanese electric Shinkansen, or "new high-speed railway," between Tokyo and Osaka was the first in the world of a new generation of high-speed railroads built exclusively for intercity passenger trains.

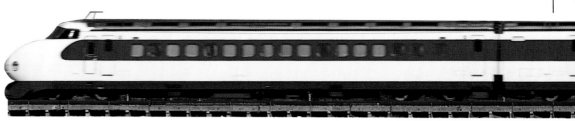

In 1965 the first regular Shinkansen service traveled at an average speed of 101 mph (163 kph), with a maximum of 130 mph (210 kph)

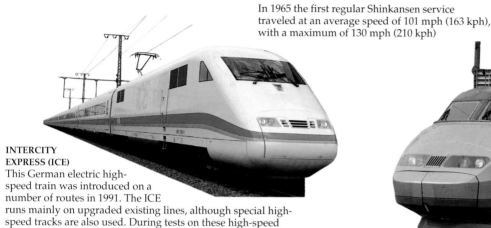

INTERCITY EXPRESS (ICE)

This German electric high-speed train was introduced on a number of routes in 1991. The ICE runs mainly on upgraded existing lines, although special high-speed tracks are also used. During tests on these high-speed lines, the ICE set a German high-speed record of 252 mph (404 kph), which was a world record for a short time.

LOCOMOTIVE NO. 999

May 10, 1893, the New York Central Railroad claimed that its steam locomotive No. 999 had become the first to exceed 100 mph (161 kph), when it reached 112.5 mph (181 kph) while working the *Empire State Express* near Batavia, New York. However, this record is no longer recognized internationally.

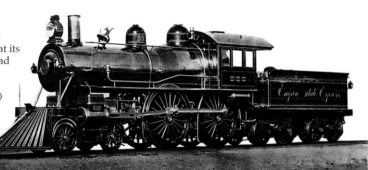

THE FASTEST EVER

The *TGV (train à grande vitesse)*, a French electric high-speed train, was introduced in 1983 between Paris and Lyon. For much of this route, the *TGV* runs on a special new track at an average speed of 131.7 mph (212 kph). In trial runs before the opening of a second high-speed line in 1990, a slightly modified *TGV* unit set a world speed record of 320 mph (515.5 kph).

STEAM RECORD

The streamlined locomotive *Mallard* was designed by British engineer Sir Nigel Gresley. On July 3, 1938, *Mallard* set a world speed record for a steam locomotive of 126 mph (203 kph). It was pulling a special train, which included a speed-recording car, down a slight grade on the main line between London and Edinburgh. This record still stands.

At the station

THE FIRST STATIONS were little more than wooden shelters next to the tracks. Passengers were able to buy tickets and wait for the train there. Today, some small rural stations are still very simple buildings, providing little more than a ticket counter and a waiting room. But where the railroad station is in a major town or city, services offered range from porters for luggage to snack bars and restaurants to parking lots to connections with road and other rail transportation. Very often, the station is the largest building in town, built on a grand scale, with imposing architecture in styles from all ages, from classical to ultra-modern.

A large clock is often the focal point of a station

COUNTRY STATION
Simple stations in rural areas often have a very low platform, or none at all. Passengers board or leave the train by climbing onto steps on the car. Trucks back up to the freight cars or use the low platform for loading and unloading.

RAILROAD TIME
For a railroad to operate successfully, trains must run on schedules. In the early days, countries with a large east-west spread, like the U.S., presented timekeeping problems. Eventually, these countries were divided into different time zones, so the time changes whenever a train crosses into a new zone.

TRANSPORTATION FOR ALL
Before road and air transportation had developed, the railroads were used for transporting all kinds of goods. This enclosed trolley was used for transporting coffins to and from the train.

GRAND CENTRAL TERMINAL
Information boards above the ticket windows show passengers where and when trains are arriving and departing. New York's Grand Central Terminal, the largest station in the world, has a huge cavernous concourse.

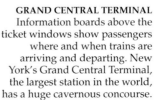

Late 19th-century
pocket watch

WATERLOO STATION
Large stations are designed so that hundreds – or even thousands – of travelers can quickly board or leave their train, all at the same time.

Simple metal whistle

WHISTLE STOP
Simple whistles made from wood or metal were used by European platform staff for communication, usually to tell the engineer when a train was ready for departure.

Railroad uniform button forms part of this British whistle

TIME IN HAND
The operation of trains to a strict timetable meant that the train crew, as well as the stations, had to have accurate timepieces. Stations had large clocks, and the crew members were provided with pocket watches.

Japanese
railway
tickets

SOUTHERN RAILWAY
PARCEL DELIVERY
SERVICE FROM
HORSTED KEYNES
STATION

SPECIAL DELIVERY
In the 1920s and 1930s the railroad provided a complete transportation service, ferrying freight to and from stations using their own road vehicles. Bicycles were used for delivering small parcels locally.

Chemin de fer de l'Iraq
Iraq Railways

Service direct entre PARIS et BASSORAH
Direct Service between PARIS and BASRA

COUPON   COUPON
pour le parcours de   for through journey from
TEL-KOTCHEK
TO
BASSORAH .. BASRA
via Mossoul par automobile à Kirguk

1ᵉ CLASSE   1ᵀᴴ CLASS

LANDMARKS
Major stations, such as the *Gare de Lyon* in Paris, were designed to provide easy access for road traffic bringing freight and passengers. Their imposing architecture made such stations a familiar landmark.

LISTEN FOR THE BELL
Handbells were rung to announce the arrival of a train in the days before electricity was available to operate electric bells.

Ticket for the
Orient Express

*London Chatham
and Dover Railway
insignia*

LC & DR
N & SW

THE ROMANCE OF STEAM
The days of steam are often portrayed as a romantic age. The classic film *Brief Encounter* is based on a chance meeting at a railway station shortly after World War II.

TICKETS PLEASE!
All around the world, passengers have to buy a ticket for their journey. Tickets are proof that a passenger has paid their fare. A conductor marks the ticket with a ticket punch so that it cannot be used again.

Running the railroad

British porter's
cap badge

Russian railroad
worker's badge

Chinese railroad
worker's badge

Great Western
Railway
fireman's
helmet

IN ADDITION TO THE FAMILIAR WORKERS - the conductors, engineers, and ticket sellers - many people are required to run a railroad. At the center of railroad activities are the commercial departments. In liaison with top management, they determine the type, frequency, and speed of the trains. It is then the job of the operating department to meet these demands. The technical engineering department must provide the necessary equipment, and the civil engineering team ensures that the track and fixed structures are in working order. All this work is supported by many specialized departments, ranging from timetabling and accounts to marketing and publicity.

OILING THE WHEELS
Steam train engineers were responsible for checking that their locomotive was in working order.

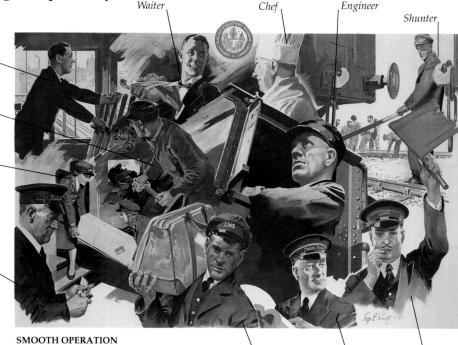

Waiter Chef Engineer Shunter

Signalman

Fireman

Porter

Ticket inspector

SMOOTH OPERATION
Railroads need a wide variety of workers in order to run smoothly. For this reason, the railroads have traditionally been among the biggest employers in many countries.

Porter Stationmaster Conductor

SAFETY FIRST
Some British railroads even ran their own fire service, trained to deal with any special hazards that might arise. The service had its own equipment and uniform.

TRAVELERS' HELPER
In the past, railroad companies owned many of the station hotels in big cities or at major junctions. The hotel porter assisted passengers arriving at or departing from the hotel.

STATIONMASTER
The stationmaster had an important role. He was in charge of all aspects of running his station and had to ensure that trains arrived and departed promptly.

When the horn was blown, the men stepped clear of the track and waited for the train to pass

Look-out man's brass horn

This horn, used in Britain, sounded a distinctive note that could not be confused with a conductor's whistle

The railroad track was known as "the right of way"

The hose is fitted into the dining car's water tank

INDISPENSABLE
Even today, with modern electrical equipment, the signal engineer has an important role, especially on busy lines. The signals on street crossings also have to be maintained. All signal equipment is designed to be "fail-safe" by displaying red stop signals if it fails to work.

TOPPING UP
In the short time that a long-distance express train stood at a station, it would have to be stocked up with enough food and water to last until the next refuelling stop. This water carrier was used to replenish the drinking-water tanks in dining cars. The tanks for the restrooms would be refilled using hoses linked to local water supplies.

"THE RIGHT OF WAY"
A great deal of organization and effort went – and still goes – into maintaining railroad track so that trains could make a safe journey. In Britain, the look-out man, in charge of the working team, would blow the horn to warn them of an approaching train.

When the wheel is turned, water is pumped through the hose

TOOLS OF THE TRADE
This oilcan was designed for filling oil lamps. The broad base makes it difficult to knock over.

Oilcan c.1890

Thick, multi-stranded wick

LIGHTING UP
Flare lamps provided light before electric battery lamps were introduced. Oil was kept in the body of the lamp and was burned at the end of the wick. The lamp warned of hazards in yards; it was also used for inspecting steam locomotives.

Oil flare lamp c.1900

The water carrier is wheeled along the platform

Still in steam

STEAM LOCOMOTIVES still operate regular passenger and freight services in parts of Asia. But in most of the world the days of steam power are a thing of the past. Cleaner, more efficient diesel and electric power represent the way forward. However, the enthusiasm felt for steam locomotives has kept them alive. Hundreds of older steam locomotives throughout the world are owned by private railroad preservation companies and are in transportation museums; many have been carefully restored to working order. They are used for pulling special trains on restored or preserved lines or on the quieter scenic lines of the national railroad networks, for tourists and enthusiasts. Occasionally, some special steam locomotives from museum collections also operate on these lines.

ALL THE GAUGES
Steam trains of all four gauges still work the main lines in India. Most narrow gauge locomotives, such as this one from India's South Eastern Railway, were imported to India from France, Germany, and Japan.

EVENING STAR below
Evening Star was the last steam locomotive built for British Rail, in 1960. It was intended for freight work but also pulled passenger and express trains in the 1960s. It was withdrawn from service in 1966. It is on display in Britain's National Railway Museum in York and still runs on special occasions.

TOURIST ATTRACTIONS
Nowadays, many steam railroads are tourist attractions. Some, such as the narrow gauge Llanberis Lake Railway in Wales (above), are modeled on working railroads that no longer exist. Others use the original routes of old railroads.

EVENING STAR

PRESERVED STEAM

The U.S. was quick to turn from steam power to diesel power. There are, however, more and more steam locomotives that have been restored to working order. Train enthusiasts can ride on some of the spectacular main-line routes, or on local lines. Steam locomotives are also displayed at museums.

Preserved locomotive of Fort Worth & Western Railroad

The building of new steam locomotives in China only ceased at the end of the 1980s

LONG LIVE STEAM

Railroads form the backbone of public transportation in China, where steam locomotives are still used extensively. At the beginning of 1990 there were some 7,000 steam locomotives, compared with 4,700 diesel and 1,200 electric.

ZIMBABWE'S STEAM REVIVAL

In the late 1970s, Zimbabwe Railways refurbished a number of their British-built Beyer-Garratt steam locomotives. This was due to the plentiful supply of Zimbabwe coal, and the desire to be independent of expensive imported oil used to fuel diesel locomotives. For this reason, Zimbabwe has attracted railroad enthusiasts from all over the world, to see and photograph some of the most powerful working steam locomotives in existence.

VETERAN LOCOMOTIVES

Relatively few lines in India and Pakistan are run especially with tourists in mind. But the wide range of steam trains still operating there, such as this 70-year-old British-built tank locomotive, attract many enthusiasts from all over the world.

All decked out

Railroads were established in the 19th century, an age familiar with elaborate decoration, so it is not surprising that they, too, were highly decorated. Imaginative displays helped to promote the services the railroad provided. Colorful signs on tunnel entrances and decorated stations also reassured the public, who were not familiar with traveling by railroad. As competition grew between the different railroad companies, decorations sporting the name of the company were applied to most railroad property, large and small. These decorations were often in the form of an ornate coat of arms or a monogram of the company's initials. Huge colorful cast-iron plaques were hung on railroad bridges, and company initials were even to be found on lanterns.

COAT OF ARMS
The ornate coat of arms of Britain's Midland Railway featured a winged monster, as well as the emblems of the major cities served by the railway.

EXPRESS TRAIN HEADBOARD
The headboard displayed the name of the train. It was fastened in front of the smokestack of the steam locomotive hauling the train.

TGV NAMEPLATE
Many of the French TGV trains' powercar units are named after cities served by these trains.

SPECIAL TRAINS
Locomotives pulling special trains were often decorated with badges or headboards created especially for the occasion.

LION CREST
This crest was displayed on British Railways locomotives and cars during the 1950s.

Boston works plate

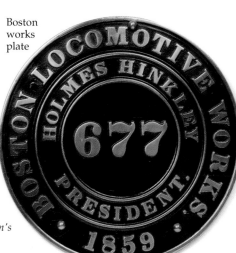

Nameplate from Britain's Southern Railway

BUILDER'S PLATE
Most locomotives carry a builder's plate, which gives the number, date, name, and very often the location of the manufacturer. This plate also carries the name of the company's president.

FAMOUS NAMES
Many locomotives have carried names of one kind or another. These have ranged from the names of contemporary and historical figures to the names of the directors of the railroad to names of places served by the railroad.

London and North Eastern Railway nameplate

The crown indicates that the railway was the only one in Canada operated with a royal charter

KNIGHT OF THE GOLDEN FLEECE
This classical name was carried by an express locomotive of Britain's Great Western Railway.

The headboard carried the name of the train

GOLD COAST RAILWAY
The coat of arms of the Gold Coast Railway featured an elephant, a familiar sight in this West African country, now known as Ghana.

NUMBER PLATE
This brass number plate is from a 1902 locomotive belonging to Canada's Dominion Atlantic Railway.

WHAT GOES WHERE?
The headboard and nameplate were carried on the locomotive. The railway company's coat of arms was displayed on the locomotive and on the cars.

GOOD PUBLICITY
Locomotives were, and still are, named after towns and cities served by the railroad, as seen in this nameplate carried by a London Midland and Scottish Railway locomotive.

Scottish flag

English flag

CALEDONIAN HEADBOARD
The shields on this headboard carry motifs of the flags of England and Scotland.

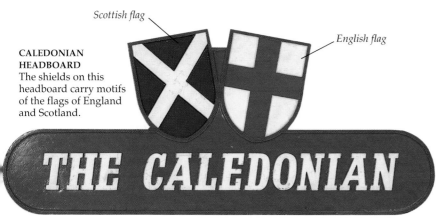

LOCAL WILDLIFE
Railroad coats of arms often incorporate images of local interest. A black swan is the symbol of the Western Australian Government Railways.

Traveling underground

THE SUCCESS OF RAILROADS in bringing people and business to the large cities also led to congestion in those cities. In London, this congestion in turn led to the building of the world's first underground railway, or subway, in 1863, connecting the main line station of Paddington to Farringdon Street in the city center. This steam-powered railroad, which ran just below the streets, was built using the "cut and cover" system – digging a trench and then covering it to form a tunnel. Despite the smoky atmosphere, it was quicker and more convenient than road travel. Later developments, such as ways of digging deeper tunnels, electric locomotives, better elevators, and escalators, allowed routes to be built deep beneath the center of London. The system became known as the "tube." The great advantages of electric underground railroads encouraged other cities around the world to develop their own subways around the end of the 19th century.

DRIVERLESS TRAINS?
Most modern rapid transit systems, such as the Metro in Washington D.C., are ideal for automation. This is because they have a steady flow of traffic, and there is no disruption by slower freight trains or faster express services. The entire network is run by a central computer-based control system, and the trains need no motormen.

OIL HAND LAMP
Hand lamps similar to this one have been used by London's conductors and signalmen for many years.

EARLY DAYS
Early impressions of the first underground steam railway show trains traveling through spacious tunnels, into which some natural light filtered. In reality, the smoke and fumes made traveling by underground train dirty and unpleasant.

LUXURY FOR ALL
The first underground railway in Moscow opened in 1933. The imposing stations were famed for their luxurious decor.

The engineer stood here

Water tank

METROPOLITAN 23 RAILWAY.

Guard rail keeps track clear of small obstacles

ALL PACKED IN
Subway cars have automatic sliding doors and wide aisles to provide as much space as possible for riders, both seated and standing.

UNIFORM BADGE
Distinctive badges worn as part of their uniform make underground railway staff easily recognizable.

London Transport badge with heraldic griffins, from early 1930s

PARIS METRO
The subway opened in Paris in 1900 and was called the *Metro*. Metro stations are very close together and easily recognizable by their signs. Any point in the city center is within comfortable walking distance of a station.

READING THE MAP
Some subway systems, such as the Paris Metro, carefully relate the route of the lines to the streets above them. This example of a London Underground map of 1927 is roughly based on a geographical map of London. Many maps used today make little attempt to do this and are not to scale.

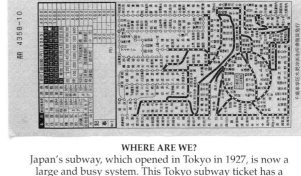

Smokestack

Pipe leading steam and smoke to water tanks

WHERE ARE WE?
Japan's subway, which opened in Tokyo in 1927, is now a large and busy system. This Tokyo subway ticket has a route map on one side.

Destination headboard

METROPOLITAN RAILWAY TANK LOCOMOTIVE
This classic underground steam locomotive was built for the Metropolitan Railway in London in 1866, only three years after the underground railway opened. To reduce the emission of smoke and steam while the train was in the tunnels, this locomotive was fitted with a valve to divert smoke and steam into its water tanks. The tanks acted as condensers, keeping the smoke and steam from blowing straight up the smokestack and overpowering passengers. Unfortunately, this technique slowed down the locomotive. To make up for lost time, engineers did not always operate the condensing equipment in the tunnels. Conditions could become very unpleasant, especially during rush hour.

Up in the air

SOME TRAINS DO NOT RUN ALONG the ground. Instead, they run on – or hang underneath – rails that are attached to overhead structures. Today, there are two such types of railway: suspended railways, where the train hangs under a rail (or rails), and "straddle" railways, where the train rides above a single rail. Suspended trains have wheels that are securely fitted onto the rails, and there is no risk of the trains falling to the ground. Trains running on the "straddle" system rest astride a single rail and are balanced and guided by wheels inside the side panels on either side of the rail. Overhead systems with a single rail are called monorails. The concept of overhead railways is not a new one. Several major cities in Europe and the U.S. operated elevated railways (conventional railways running on overhead tracks) by the end of the 19th century, and a monorail has been used in Germany since 1901. Modern overhead railways are less expensive to build than conventional railways. They offer passengers a good view and avoid conflict with ground traffic, something neither conventional rail nor road systems can offer. Like conventional electric trains, modern overhead trains do not pollute the air. They are, however, very prominent and many consider them to be an eyesore; they are also noisier than street trains because of their elevated position.

NEW YORK'S ELEVATED TRAIN
Toward the end of the 19th century, as street congestion in large cities grew, elevated railways were seen as a cheaper and more flexible alternative to underground subways. This elevated city railway was built in New York in the 1880s.

Second track for cars going in opposite direction

MONTMARTRE FUNICULAR
Funicular railways are a special form of cable railway, used for raising or lowering loads on steep ground over relatively short distances. They were originally developed with a double track for freight work. The cable system was balanced so that loaded cars descending on one line helped to pull up empty or partly loaded cars on the adjacent line. Most funiculars are now electrically powered and carry passengers rather than freight. The cars are attached to a common cable, and neither can move until both ascending and descending trains are ready. This funicular line in Paris, France, was built in 1900 and is still operating today, with new cars.

OUT OF THE WAY
The compact and flexible nature of a monorail system makes it ideal for a wide variety of uses. Monorails, such as this one at the National Motor Museum at Beaulieu, England, have often been used to transport visitors around exhibitions and theme parks. Because they are elevated, these railways can cover ground crowded with pedestrians without causing any obstruction.

GLASGOW "SAIL PLANE"

This "sail plane" was developed in the 1920s by George Bennie and tested near Glasgow, Scotland. It was a suspended monorail that traveled along a track using a propeller similar to those used on airplanes. The motor to drive the propeller could be either diesel or electric. Despite the usual advantages of an overhead railway, the "sail plane" was not developed beyond the experimental stage.

NOVELTY VALUE

Monorails have great novelty value and are frequently used in theme parks. This small lightweight open-car monorail operates in a Dutch zoo, where animals can be viewed and photographed in complete safety.

THE FIRST MONORAIL

The first commercial monorail opened in Wuppertal, in northwest Germany, in 1901 and is still in operation today. The electric trains are suspended beneath the rail. For much of its 8-mile (12.9-km) journey, the railway straddles the Wupper river.

Monorails travel
on a single rail,
or beam

Power line

Side web of rail

TRAIN WITH ONE RAIL

Most modern monorails, such as this one (exhibited in Brisbane, Australia, at the Expo '90 fair), are designed so that the car straddles the supporting structure. It is balanced and guided by side panels that contain guide wheels. The car runs on electric power, which is collected from conductor strips set in the side webs of the rail, or beam. Monorails are also used in permanent locations – the train from Tokyo to Haneda Airport, Japan, a distance of 8 miles (13 km), is a monorail.

Supporting beam

Trains for fun

No SOONER HAD RAILROADS been invented for transportation than people began to build them, in one form or the other, for amusement. These trains ranged from simple toys for children to push on the floor to highly detailed operating models. The earliest toy trains were made of flat pieces of lead; then came wooden trains with rotating wheels. By the latter half of the 19th century, wood models had given way to tinplate trains running on model tracks, driven at first by clockwork, like a wind-up alarm clock, and later by electricity. As manufacturing techniques improved, models became more detailed to satisfy the demand for greater accuracy. The traditional children's toy increasingly became the more sophisticated miniature scale model of the enthusiast and collector. But whether simple toys or miniature scale models, toy trains still fascinate children and adults alike.

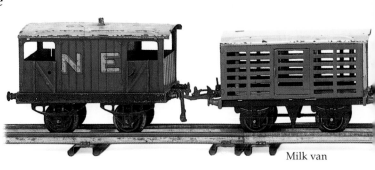

Milk van

These images are cut out and made into three-dimensional locomotives

CUT AND PASTE
Miniature cardboard cutout "do-it-yourself" models are an alternative and cheaper way of collecting models of famous locomotives. This example was advertised as "a workshop in a cigar box".

SMALLER THAN LIFE
Miniature trains on which children and adults can ride are built just for entertainment. They have been popular since the 19th century, especially when pulled by steam engines.

GRAND JUNCTION RAILWAY LOCOMOTIVE
This precision-engineered model is of a classic freight locomotive design dating from 1846. A good model like this has all the features of a full-size train in working order – such as oil lamps, levers, and whistles.

THE PERFECT PRESENT
Train sets have always made ideal gifts for children of all ages. A basic train set can be built up to include stations, bridges, tunnels, signals, and all the elements of a modern railroad.

1930s freight train set

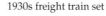

TIN-PLATE TRAINS
British tin-plate clockwork train sets were well made and reasonably durable. Such sets included lengths of track and sometimes other accessories, such as switches, stations, and tunnels.

Tanker wagon

Cement wagon

PRECISION-MADE MODEL
Models are often made of famous locomotives, such as this mass-produced but detailed model of a heavy freight steam locomotive built in the early 1940s for the Union Pacific Railroad. Although this model uses mostly metal materials, well-molded plastics are more often used today to provide more accurate detail and to reduce costs.

BOARD GAMES
The railroads had such a huge impact on society that the train theme appeared in many aspects of everyday life. Even family games, such as this French board game of the 1870s, featured the railroad.

THOMAS THE TANK ENGINE
Both paintings and photographs of railroad scenes have been widely used for jigsaw puzzles. This puzzle features Thomas the Tank Engine, the main character in a series of children's books written by the Reverend Awdry in the 1940s.

"LADY OF LYNN"
Accurate working scale models are usually made as a hobby by skilled craftsmen. This coal-fired working model is of an express locomotive that ran on the Great Western Railway in Britain in 1908.

Into the future

RAILROADS HAVE PROVED their worth in so many areas that their future is guaranteed. New kinds of trains and track are being developed, and existing equipment is constantly being improved. In addition to easing city congestion and pollution, railroads provide swift, comfortable cross-country transportation. New, faster, more comfortable electric trains are being introduced in several countries, from Europe to Asia. For more passenger comfort, tilting high-speed trains can now be used on traditional lines, avoiding the extra cost of building special new tracks. Rail freight services have lost a lot of business to road transportation. However, the benefits to the environment and to overcrowded highways, together with improved techniques for carrying freight by rail, suggest a halt to these losses. In cities, similar environmental concerns have led to the construction of many new electric rapid transit systems. Such developments will help to improve links between road, rail, and air travel.

This maglev train service opened in Birmingham, England, in the mid-1980s. It operates over a distance of 2,034 ft (620 m) between the airport and Birmingham's International Railway Station.

MAGNETIC LEVITATION
This maglev train works by *magnetic levitation*. Instead of traveling on wheels on a track, the passenger car (which has no wheels) hovers up to 0.78 in (2 cm) above a metal track and is pulled along by magnets. This system has many advantages – there are no moving parts to wear out, no maintenance is required, and it makes hardly any noise. Maglev trains are still being developed to run at very high speeds.

The Docklands Light Railway is elevated above street level

DRIVERLESS TRAINS
Light rail transit systems, such as the Docklands Light Railway in London (left), provide a convenient and frequent service in congested city centers. The trains are powered by electricity, which is collected from a shielded third rail along the track. There are no engineers, the trains are operated automatically by computer from a central control room.

TRIED AND FAILED
The development of the gas turbine engine soon attracted the interest of railroad engineers. The first gas turbine locomotive was built for Swiss Railways in 1941. This picture shows a Canadian National Railways gas turbine-powered train. Like many trains of its kind, it proved to be unreliable and was withdrawn from service in the mid-1980s.

SUPER TRAIN
Eurostar international passenger trains operate from London between Paris and Brussels, via the Channel Tunnel which was opened in 1994. The specially built high speed Eurostars can take power from four different systems and reach speeds of 186 mph (300 kph). Nearly 1,220 ft (400 m) long, they can carry 770 passengers in comfort during a journey time of around three hours from city centre to city centre.

Eurostar Passenger train

TAKING THE BEND
Tilting trains developed by the Italian Railways have recently been designed to provide high-speed service on upgraded traditional lines. When a curve is detected by the sensor controls, the train is tilted by a hydraulic mechanism to ensure passenger comfort as the train goes through the curve. These electric trains have a maximum speed of 155 mph (250 kph). At present these trains operate on several routes in Italy.

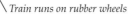
Train runs on rubber wheels

Steel rail guides train

"PEOPLE MOVER"
This relatively simple rapid transit system has been used successfully in airports in the U.S. and in England. The trains run on rubber tires along a concrete track. They are guided by a central steel rail, which also carries the power for the electric motors. These trains are driverless – all operations, such as speed, braking, and the opening and closing of doors, are controlled by a central computer. They are ideal for the short journey from one airport terminal to another, traveling at speeds of up to 26 mph (41 kph).

Wheels run on concrete track

Index

Acknowledgments

Dorling Kindersley would like to thank:
All the staff at the National Railway Museum, York, especially David Wright and Richard Gibbon.
John Liffen at the Science Museum.
Justin Scobie for photographic assistance.
The London Transport Museum.
The signal box staff of Three bridges (British Rail) Station, West Sussex.
The Bluebell Railway.
Gatwick Airport.
Claire Gillard for initial research.
Helena Spiteri and Gin von Noorden for editorial assistance.
Earl Neish for design assistance.
Jane Parker for the index.

Picture credits

t=top, b=bottom, c=center, l=left, r=right

Front cover: Peter Newark's Picture Library
Advertising Archives: 26bc, 61tl (detail), 61tr (detail)
Australian Overseas Information Service, London: 42cl
Barlow Reid: 7acr, 39cr, 41cr
Bettmann Archive Hulton Picture Library: 19t, 20c
Bridgeman Art Library/Science Museum, London: 11btc National Railway Museum, York:11tr; /Private Collections: 13btc; / Guildhall Art Gallery, Corporation of London: 45cl; /Guildhall Library, Corporation of London: 56cl;
Britt Allcroft (Thomas Ltd): 1989: 61cl
Channel Tunnel: 63cr

Jean-Loup Charmet: 10bcr, 30bl, 39tr, 44cl, 56cr
J.A.Coiley 54cr, 58br
G Cooke, Rail Safaris: 53cl
Culver Pictures Inc: 11tl, 16btr, 19br, 37tl, 41btr, 47btr
Michael Dent: 23cl, 52c, 55cr
Docklands Light Railway Ltd/Marysha Alwan: 62b et archive: 6c, 7cl, 9tl,9tc, 9cl, 12cl, 16bl, 20tr, 26btr(detail), 28tr, 29cr, 33btc, 36tr, 46cl, 49bcl, 51tr
Mary Evans Picture Library: 8br, 9cr, 13t, 17btl, 21bcl, 29tl, 35tc, 38c, 40tl, 61bcr
Ffotograff: 42tr
Robert Harding Picture Library: 52cl 58bl, 59cy
Hulton Picture Company: 31btl
Hutchison Picture Library: 22tl, 53tr
Antony J Lambert: 45c, 60cl
Mansell Collection Ltd: 8tr, 10acr, 23tc
John Massey Stewart: 45bcl, 56tr, 59nr
Millbrook House Ltd: 7tr, 23br, 37tr,

51btl, 58cr, 63tr
National Railway Museum: 6cl, 7tl, 12tr, 13btr, 21tl, 21tr, 23tr, 25tr,25bcr, 26bcl, 30bc, 35cr, 37btc, 43bcr, 49tc, 50cr, 59tl; / Terrence Cuneo: 33bc;
Peter Newark's Picture Library: 13c, 18tl, 18cr, 19c, 19tr, 24tr, 34tl, 42bl, 43br, 53btl
Quadrant Picture Library: 21c, 27btc, 35br, 43btr, 47btl, 47c, 53cr, 62tr
Rank Films: 49bl
Retrograph Archive/Martin Breese: 36tl
Mack Sennet Productions: 25btr
Telegraph Colour Library: 50tr, 57c
La Vie du Rail, Paris: 38cl, 39tl, 63tl
Weintraub/Ronald Grant: 31tl
Zefa Picture Library 24tl, 35tl, 41tr, 47t, 48br, 59b
Every effort has been made to trace the copyright holders. Dorling Kindersley apologises for any unintentional ommissions and would be pleased, in such cases to add an acknowledgement in future editions.

1 BIRD

2 ROCKS & MINERALS

3 SKELETON

4 ARMS & ARMOR

5 TREE

6 POND & RIVER

7 BUTTERFLY & MOTH

8 SPORTS

9 SHELL

10 EARLY HUMANS

11 MAMMAL

12 MUSIC

13 DINOSAUR

14 PLANT

15 SEASHORE

16 FLAG

17 INSECT

18 MONEY

19 FOSSIL

20 FISH

21 CAR

22 FLYING MACHINE

23 ANCIENT EGYPT

24 ANCIENT ROME

25 CRYSTAL & GEM

26 REPTILE

27 INVENTION

28 WEATHER

29 CAT

30 BIBLE LANDS

31 EXPLORER

32 DOG

33 HORSE

34 FILM

35 COSTUME

36 BOAT

37 ANCIENT GREECE

38 VOLCANO & EARTHQUAKE

39 TRAIN

40 SHARK

41 AMPHIBIAN

42 ELEPHANT

43 KNIGHT

44 MUMMY

45 COWBOY

46 WHALE

47 AZTEC, INCA & MAYA

48 BOOK

49 CASTLE

50 VIKING

51 DESERT

52 PREHISTORIC LIFE

53 PYRAMID

54 JUNGLE

55 ANCIENT CHINA

56 ARCHEOLOGY

57 ARCTIC & ANTARCTIC

58 BUILDING

59 PIRATE

60 NORTH AMERICAN INDIAN

61 AFRICA

62 OCEAN

63 BATTLE

64 GORILLA, MONKEY & APE

65 MEDIEVAL LIFE

66 FARM

67 SPY

68 RELIGION

69 EAGLE & BIRDS OF PREY

70 WITCHES & MAGIC-MAKERS

71 SPACE EXPLORATION

72 SHIPWRECK